THIS PRESIDENT
101 Reasons
to
Re-Elect Donald Trump

J. Preta Simon

This President: 101 Reasons to Re-Elect Donald Trump

Published 2020 in the United States by Discovery Docx

ISBN 9798692634436 (p)

Contents

2021 Note: Sources may be found at the President Trump Administration Archives

https://www.archives.gov/presidential-libraries/archived-websites

https://trumpwhitehouse.archives.gov/

Introduction

This book looks at statistics, public sources, and registered documents to show what President Donald Trump has done since he was elected president in 2016. There are more than 500 reasons, but the top 101 are listed here.

They are in no particular order, but the top ten or twenty are vital to America's future as a nation; many of the rest are to keep Americans productive, healthy, and ready to reach their individual aspirations.

For a few moments, forget the fluff and screaming of social media, cable news, and shouting radio stations and podcasts. Read the reasons, check out the links in Sources. See how President Trump's record stacks up to what you want in the next president.

Reason 1. President Trump Listens

As soon as President Donald J. Trump took office, he began listening to experts and workers in their fields. He held listening sessions with educators, business owners large and small, policy makers, social advocates, and health leaders. In preparation to remove the Affordable Care Act (Obamacare), President Trump held listening sessions with health insurance representatives like Brad Wilson (president and CEO of Blue Cross and Blue Shield of North Carolina), Bruce Broussard (CEO of Humana), and Joe Swedish (with Anthem).

To understand how better to serve African Americans and Black Americans, he listened to voices representing Historically Black Colleges and Universities, and Dr. Ben Carson, Paris Dennard, Pastor Darrell Scott, Gerard Robinson (American Enterprise Institute), and Leah LeVell to discover their needs. He also held listening sessions with retail industry leaders, police organizations, numerous federal agencies on how to stop human trafficking, the Veterans Administration, National Economic Council, small business owners, leaders in the agricultural fields, mayors, and steel and aluminum representatives in the first few months of his administration.

He continued to listen, too, meeting and holding roundtable discussions with law enforcement and border patrol agents about security, gang activity, and sanctuary cities, and hosted a roundtable to meet with tribal and state leaders regarding energy opportunities. To get a closer look at how to lift the economy, he met with automakers and other representatives from Nissan North America, Nissan North America, Alliance of Automobile Manufacturers, Duluth Seaway Port Authority, Iron Mining Association of Minnesota, Pfizer, Merck, and Novartis. He also held listening sessions on prison reform, state and national defense, and Hispanic pastors and Hispanic job makers and political leaders.

President Trump listened, and then he took action on what he heard.

Reason 2. Constitutional Judges

President Trump promised to put Constitutional judges on the Supreme Court, further solidifying America's true foundations as outlined by its Founders.

By mid-December of his first year in office, President Trump crossed the all-time record with Senate confirming his twelfth federal appeals court nominee.

By September 2, 2020, the U.S. Senate had confirmed 203 Article III judges nominated by President Trump, including two associate justices of the Supreme Court of the United States, 53 judges for U.S. courts of appeals, 146 judges for U.S. district courts, and two judges for the United States Court of International Trade. At that time, 42 nominations to Article III courts were awaiting Senate action, including 41 for district courts and one for the Court of International Trade. There were currently 70 vacancies on the U.S. district courts and two vacancies on the U.S. Court of International Trade (September 2020).

On March 10, 2017, Neil McGill Gorsuch was added to the Supreme Court of the United States as an Associate Justice, President Trump's choice. President Trump nominee Brett M.

Kavanaugh was seated as Associate Justice of the U.S. Supreme Court on October 6, 2018, following tetchy Democrat harassment during his confirmation.

On September 19, 2020, Associate Justice Ruth Bader Ginsberg died, having served 27 years on the U.S. Supreme Court. President Trump began the process of choosing a third nominee judge for the Supreme Court. Shortly after Justice Ginsberg's death, Senate Majority Leader Mitch McConnell stated the Senate would put a vote to the floor before the end of President Trump's first term if the President sent a nominee. On October 26, 2020, President Trump put forth Amy Coney Barrett as his nominee for the Supreme Court.

Reason 3. Protecting Free Speech

In March 2019, President Trump signed Executive Order EO 13798-Promoting Free Speech and Religious Liberty, and Executive Order EO 13925-Preventing Online Censorship in May 2020, to protect free speech in America and online. These maintained freedom of expression and religious beliefs and expression, even online in a time of social platforms and social media companies attempting to censor opinions. This included taking suitable steps to ensure college and university campuses offer free thought and debate environments for all views.

Reason 4. Religious Rights

On May 9, 2017, President Trump signed Executive Order EO 13798-Promoting Free Speech and Religious Liberty, safeguarding religious freedom, religious speech, and political speech, shoring up our First Amendment rights. On February 21, 2018, President Trump signed Proclamation 9698-Death of Billy Graham and Statement on the Death of Billy Graham upon the reverend's passing, to commemorate the religious leader that had served numerous administrations.

President Trump acknowledges the power of faith in communities and values the women and men in service. In May 2018, President Trump signed Executive Order EO 13831-Establishment of a White House Faith and Opportunity Initiative, in hopes of faith-based organizations being instrumental in aiding civil society, lifting people up, keeping families strong, and solving problems on the local level.

In August 2018, President Trump met with inner city pastors, including Pastor Paula White, Bishop Harry Jackson, and Dr. Alveda King, Dr. Van Moody, Bishop Kyle Searcy, Pastor Benny Perez, former prisoner Pastor Jon Ponder, and Pastor Darrell Scott, among others, to discuss the importance of religious outreach in distressed communities. The focus was on mentoring, post-prison training, and local community revitalization and what the Trump Administration can do to help them reach their goals.

To protect religious liberties, President Trump approved S. 994 / Public Law No. 115–249 Protecting Religiously Affiliated Institutions Act of 2018. This modified an existing prohibition in the federal criminal code regarding intentionally obstructing (by force or threat of force) a person's free exercise of religious beliefs. This threat of force includes religious real property (including real property owned or leased by a nonprofit, religiously affiliated organization). This was backed by a criminal penalty (fine, prison term of up to three years, or both) for a violation resulting in damage or destruction to religious real property where the amount exceeds $5,000. (Sponsored by Senator Orrin G. Hatch, R-UT.)

Reason 5. The Second Amendment

On April 28, 2017, at the National Rifle Association Leadership Forum at the Georgia World Conference Center in Atlanta, President Trump stated plainly, when referring to Senator David Perdue and Senator Ted Cruz, "We all took an oath to preserve, protect, and defend the Constitution of the United States—and that means defending the Second Amendment. So let me make a simple promise to every one of the freedom-loving Americans in the audience today: As your President, I will never, ever infringe on the right of the people to keep and bear arms. Never ever. Freedom is not a gift from government. Freedom is a gift from God."

Reason 6. Pro-Life and Protecting the Unborn

Less abortion. On January 23, 2017, President Trumps signed a Presidential Memorandum Regarding the Mexico City Policy, banning U.S. aid from supporting organizations that perform or endorse abortions. The "Protecting Life in Global Health Assistance Initiative" broadened this policy. This revoked the Presidential Memorandum of January 23, 2009, for the Secretary of State and the Administrator of the United States Agency for International Development (Mexico City Policy and Assistance for Voluntary Population Planning), and reinstated the Presidential Memorandum of January 22, 2001, for the Administrator of the United States Agency for International Development (Restoration of the Mexico City Policy).

On April 13, 2017, President Trump signed H.J. Res 43, allowing states to withhold Title X grant money from Planned Parenthood and other abortion providers (sponsored by Representative Diane Black, R-TN). Also in April 2017, President Trump suspended taxpayer funding for the U.N. Population Fund (UNPFA) that supported China's cruel program of forced abortion and sterilization, which violated the 1985 Kemp-Kasten amendment. As of June 5, 2019, President Trump ended Federal research using fetal tissue from abortions and refused renewing further research.

In January 2020, President Trump became the first sitting president to attend the annual March for Life in Washington, DC. President Trump spoke at the 47th Annual March for Life, stating, ". . . the movement is led by strong women, amazing faith leaders, and brave students who carry on the legacy of pioneers before us who fought to raise the conscience of our nation and uphold the rights of our citizens. You embrace mothers with care and compassion. You are powered by prayer, and motivated by pure, unselfish love."

In February 2020, President Trump continued to fight for the unborn. He supported the Pain-Capable Unborn Child Protection Act, which would halt late-term abortions after 20 weeks of pregnancy (sponsored by Senator Lindsey Graham, R-SC; bill is still in Senate (Sept. 2020)). And in late September 2020, President Trump signed an Executive Order on Protecting Vulnerable Newborn and Infant Children in response to the *post*-birth "abortion" procedure used in some clinics.

Reason 7. Reining in Regulations

In early 2017, President Trump signed Presidential Memorandum Reducing Regulatory Burdens for Domestic Manufacturing, expediting manufacturing and constructions reviews and permits, thus speeding up job openings. Without the shackles of business-killing regulations, the economy had more opportunities to flourish. Before 2018, President Trump's Administration surpassed the 2:1 ratio on deregulation, eliminating 22 regulations for every new regulation created.

This enabled more businesses to start, and existing businesses to thrive.

In April 2017, President Trump signed Executive Order EO 13789-Identifying and Reducing Tax Regulatory Burdens, setting up a committee to look into onerous regulations stopping employers from hiring and expanding businesses. Overreaching regulations had stifled business growth, kept small businesses from expanding, and driven larger companies out of the U.S. Deregulation allowed more businesses to open, grow, and hire new workers.

President Trump continued to lift constraints on job growth in March 2018 by approving H.R. 1177 / Public Law No. 115–156 Removing Outdated Restrictions to Allow for Job Growth Act (sponsored by Representative Bruce Poliquin, R-ME).

In May 2018, President Trump's deregulation agenda included regulatory reform to help small businesses and commercial fishermen in the Pacific Ocean, examination of problematic prescription rules, and aid in lifting regulations for infrastructure, energy, and space programs.

Reason 8. Building the Wall

The U.S.-Mexico border Wall gets built. Candidate Trump promised a wall along the U.S.-Mexico border, and that wall is going up. Despite battling Congress and special interest groups and rogue judges, by July 2019, the Department of Homeland Security (DHS) and U.S. Customs and Border Protection (CBP) oversaw construction of the border wall along the U.S.-Mexico border (new bollard wall), including gates, in San Diego, El Centro, El Paso, and the Rio Grande Valley Sectors priority areas.

By late 2018, $1.375 billion was allotted for border wall construction (FY2018), and approximately 84 miles of border wall was erected in several locations stretching across the Southwest border. The funds went to: $251 million for a secondary border wall (San Diego Sector); $445 million to construct a new levee wall system (Rio Grande Valley Sector); $196 million to construct a new steel bollard wall system (Rio Grande Valley Sector); $445 million for a primary pedestrian wall (San Diego, El Centro, Yuma, Tucson Sectors). Despite partisan bickering, future plans are to use the remaining funds from FY2017 and FY2018, plus any monies from FY2019 for the DHS in the following areas (using $5 billion as a forecast): five miles (San Diego Sector, CA); 14 miles (El Centro Sector, CA); 27 miles (Yuma Sector, AZ); nine miles (El Paso Sector, NM New); 55 miles (Laredo Sector, TX); and 104 miles (Rio Grande Valley Sector, TX), for a total of 215 miles of the needed 330 miles. These are the areas considered the highest priorities by the Border Patrol at the time.

President Trump continued with his promise to "Build the Wall" into 2020. By June 2020, according to the CBP, construction of more than 200 miles of new border wall system were completed. Dilapidated and outdated sections of previously existing barrier were replaced. By September 14, 2020, over 320 miles of wall were built, integrated with existing barriers, and utilized natural barriers like rivers and impassible terrain. (See the video to watch work done. https://www.cbp.gov/border-security/along-us-borders/border-wall-system)

President Trump's promise to bring safety along the U.S.-Mexico border is kept.

Reason 9. The COVID-19 Shutdown Decision

In mid-March 2020, President Trump made the difficult but necessary decision to close the U.S. borders and effectively halt the full-throttle economy he had built over the last three years. COVID-19 had come to America's shores and was sweeping through New York City.

President Trump put Vice President Pence in charge of the White House Coronavirus Task Force, which consisted of Dr. Anthony Fauci (Director of the National Institute of Allergy and Infectious Diseases) and Dr. Deborah Birx (Coronavirus Response Coordinator for the White House Coronavirus Task Force). Vice President Pence outlined to the public a "15 Days to Slow the Spread" of the virus plan. Life came to a halt as schools, businesses, factories, stores, and shops closed, restaurants were relegated to take-out only, and nearly every door closed to the public. States outlined what businesses could remain open—essential businesses with only essential workers—and America's streets and roads stretched empty across cities and countrysides. Some state officials—seeing the opportunity to seize previously untouchable power over their states—took that fifteen days and extended it (to the date of this writing). The booming economy President Trump had so carefully built winked out of sight in hours.

President Trump's tough call to shut down the U.S. economy was devastating to watch. However, this downslide was not the culmination of bad business decisions, outsourced jobs, slow demand for products and services, or an ill-equipped workforce. And President Trump left the keys in the door for business to resume quickly once the virus was under control in the form of the Paycheck Protection Program (PPP). By lending forgivable loans to companies to keep their staffs and employees on payroll during the epidemic close, businesses had a ready "turn-key" switch left *on* to reopen.

While fighting with Congress to pass the needed stimulus packages for American families and the PPP for businesses (slowed by Democratic fluff pushed into the bill, with the House still smarting over the Senate's *Nay* votes on impeaching President Trump during this time), President Trump also geared American companies for an all-hands approach to combating the virus. He met with business leaders to suppress the virus, keep food on American tables, and stock personal protection needs in medical facilities, while eyeing the future on how to safely reopen the country.

Reason 10. Removing the Obamacare Mandate

Less Obamacare. On January 20, 2017, President Trump signed Executive Order EO 13765-Minimizing the Economic Burden of the Patient Protection and Affordable Care Act Pending Repeal (ACA, Obamacare). This took the teeth—the forced compliance and monetary punishment—out of compulsory participation. Companies, and individuals, were free to find better and less expensive healthcare without getting slapped with large fines upon filing income tax returns.

President Trump followed this up by releasing details, including covering preexisting conditions, on the America-First Healthcare Plan in September 2020.

Reason 11. President Trump Signs GOP Tax Reform Bill

On December 22, 2017, President Trump signed H.R. 1 / Public Law No. 115–97, the GOP Tax Cuts and Jobs Act of 2017 (TCJA) (sponsored by Representative Kevin Brady (R-TX)). This cut taxes, allowing U.S. companies to repatriate money held offshore at a tax holiday level, opening up more employment opportunities. These were all points the President had campaigned on, and now they were official. The ensuing confidence in the economy was immediately felt.

At President Trump's prompting, the GOP had worked on the tax bill to restructure individual income brackets and entice businesses back to American shores, and companies responded, even before President Trump signed. Big business in America readied to charge full steam forward under the tax break. AT&T stated it would pay a $1,000 bonus to over 200,000 U.S. employees after the GOP tax bill was enacted. It also planned to invest an additional $1 billion in the United States in 2018.

In December 2017, as a result of the bill passing, Boeing committed an additional $300 million in investments, including $100 million for corporate giving in charitable areas such as employee gift-matching, education, communities, veterans and military personnel, and $100 million for workforce development in training and education, and $100 million for workplace facilities and infrastructure upgrades for Boeing employees.

As confidence with the new lower tax rungs spread across the U.S., some companies celebrated by giving back to employees. A week before Christmas 2018, in Ludington, Michigan, the owner of FloraCraft announced bonuses to 200 employees in the form of cash and a special gift to 401(k) plans, totaling $4 million. Based on time on the job, employees received an average of $20,000. The average employee had been with the company for nine years, but some were second- and third-generation employees. Those with forty years of tenure received $60,000 in bonuses.

In response to the 2017 GOP tax bill, Fifth Third Bancorp said it would hike its minimum hourly wage to $15, which would benefit 3,000 hourly employees, and give out a one-time bonus of $1,000 to about 75 percent of its employees. Comcast NBC Universal stated it would award $1,000 special bonuses to over 100,000 eligible frontline and non-executive employees, contingent upon the repeal of net neutrality. The company also pledged to invest $50 billion within the next five years in infrastructure.

In the weeks following the GOP 2017 tax bill passage and into 2018, companies from a vast array of businesses stepped up. Now paying less in business taxes, companies shared the wealth. Citing President Trump's new tax law, companies announced bonuses, pay raises, voluntary minimum wage increases, stock grants, and other employee benefits; included were Kansas City Southern, PNC Financial Services, Melaleuca Inc., Aquesta Financial Holdings, First Hawaiian Bank, Bank of Hawaii, AAON, AccuWeather, Aflac, American Airlines, Bank of the Ozarks, BB&T, Citizens Financial Group, Comerica Bank, Copperleaf Assisted Living, Dayton T. Brown Inc., Express Employment Professionals, JetBlue, National Bank Holdings Corporation, Navient, Southwest Airlines, The Flood Insurance Agency, Turning Point Brands, Wal-Mart, AT&T, Boeing, Comcast, Wells Fargo, Fifth Third Bancorp, Alaska Air Group, HomeStreet, Inc. (Seattle), Starbucks Coffee Company, The Home Depot, Lowe's, Dollar Tree, U-Haul, FedEx, McDonald's, Mill Steel Company, WebHobby Shop, LLC., and many more. In early 2018, Fiat Chrysler Automobiles also gave back. FCA gave out bonuses of $2,000 to 60,000 employees (salaried and hourly).

The run up to the end of 2017 was a race to full employment as confidence in the future spread across the country. National Association of Manufacturers' (NAM) Outlook Survey for the third quarter of 2017 indicated strong levels of confidence in business conditions year-to-date, up from 60.8 in the second quarter to 61.0 in the third quarter. For comparison, the index had been at 41.3 a year ago. With the prospects of the GOP's revised tax bill, companies reported they would use their increase in capital to expand their businesses (64.3 percent), hire more workers (57.3 percent), increase employee wages and benefits (52.2 percent), and invest more in their community (34.2 percent).

When the bill passed as 2017 came to a close, those companies were ready to give back, pay more, hire anew, and expand their businesses. Within a year, President Trump had gotten U.S. manufacturing on its feet and racing into the future.

Reason 12. U.S. Energy Independence

While "America First" never meant *America alone*, becoming energy independent liberated the U.S. from relying on foreign countries—some not so friendly—and allowed change to foreign policy in America's favor.

In April 2017, President Trump signed Executive Order EO 13795-Implementing an America-First Offshore Energy Strategy, to seek new areas of energy discovery "while ensuring that any such activity is safe and environmentally responsible."

The Trump Administration's focus on deregulation and innovation took energy dominance to new levels. Innovations in this sector benefitted Americans by boosting productivity and reducing energy prices for consumers. By the end of 2018, the U.S. surpassed China and Russia to become the world's largest oil-exporting leader. Soon after, America became a net exporter of petroleum products (crude oil and refined) for the first time since 1949. By 2019, the U.S. was energy independent for the first time in over 60 years.

In April 2019, President Trump signed Executive Order EO 13868-Promoting Energy Infrastructure and Economic Growth to ensure safety regarding energy and sources, emphasizing innovation over heavy regulations in petroleum, oil, liquid natural gas, and coal.

Reason 13. USMCA Trade

In mid-August 2017, President Trump began renegotiating the North American Free Trade Agreement (NAFTA) with Canada and Mexico for better terms for the U.S.'s interests. This would later become the United States Mexico Canada Agreement (USMCA). News of how USMCA, which replaced the existing NAFTA, was broken down by state on October 18, 2018, showing how each would be affected. (See Reason 13 "States" in Sources to see how your state is affected.)

Over the course of late November and early December 2018, President Trump further negotiated the trade Agreement between the United States of America, the United Mexican States, and Canada. This helped equalize trade between the three countries, a long-time interest of President Trump. (To see the schedule of tariffs between Canada, Mexico, and the U.S., see Reason 13 "Trade" in Sources.)

As the details were worked out, the lopsided trade of the former NAFTA sharpened focus. By December 20, 2019, the new trade deal President Trump had brokered was met with enthusiasm by members of Congress, advocacy and policy organizations, cabinet members, administration officials, and state officials. Among those welcoming the new deal:

House Minority Leader Kevin McCarthy (R-CA)
House Majority Whip Jim Clyburn (D-SC)
House Minority Whip Steve Scalise (R-LA)
Senate Finance Committee Chairman Chuck Grassley (R-IA)
Sen. Deb Fischer (R-NE)
Rep. Josh Harder (D-CA)
Rep. Cindy Axne (D-IA)
Rep. Susan Brooks (R-IN)
Rep. Mike Johnson (R-LA)
Rep. Don Bacon (R-NE)
Rep. Steven Horsford (D-NV)

Rep. Dan Meuser (R-PA)
Rep. Henry Cuellar (D-TX)
Rep. Don Beyer (D-VA)
Rep. Abigail Spanberger (D-VA)
Governor Kim Reynolds (R-IA)
Governor Larry Hogan (R-MD)
Secretary of Agriculture Mike Naig (R-IA)
California State Senator Shannon Grove (R-CA)
Secretary of Agriculture Sonny Perdue
Secretary of Commerce Wilbur Ross
United States Trade Representative Robert Lighthizer
United States Permanent Representative to the United Nations Amb. Kelly Craft
American Automotive Policy Council President Former Missouri Governor Matt Blunt
American Beverage Association President and CEO Katherine Lugar
American Chemistry Council President and CEO Chris Jahn
American Farm Bureau Federation President Zippy Duvall
American Trucking Association President and CEO Chris Spear
Association of American Railroads President and CEO Ian Jefferies
Association of Equipment Manufacturers President Dennis Slater
BSA The Software Alliance
Business Roundtable Trade and International Committee Chair Tom Linebarger
Corn Refiners Association President and CEO John Bode
Farmers for Free Trade Co-Executive Director Angela Hofmann
General Motors
International Dairy Foods Association President and CEO Michael Dykes
National Association of Home Builders Chairman Greg Ugalde
National Association of Manufacturers President and CEO Jay Timmons
National Chicken Council President Mike Brown

National Corn Growers Association President Kevin Ross
National Council of Textiles President and CEO Kim Glas
National Milk Producers Federation President and CEO Jim Mulhern
National Retail Federation President and CEO Matthew Shay
National Turkey Federation
SBE Council President & CEO Karen Kerrigan
Trade Works For America Co-Chair Phil Cox
United States Chamber of Commerce CEO Thomas J. Donohue
United States Dairy Export Council President and CEO Tom Vilsack
United States Travel Association

Among the changes in the new deal were that 75% of each qualifying vehicles must be produced in North America, 40% to 45% of the vehicle must be built by labor paid at least $16/hour, and unfair restrictions (by Canada) on American dairy, wheat, and wine producers were lifted.

In September 2020, even former vice president and presidential candidate Joe Biden admitted in a CNN interview that President Trump's USMCA trade deal was better for Americans than NAFTA.

Reason 14. Support for Veterans and VA

After a listening session with veteran advocates and U.S. Secretary of Veterans Affairs David Shulkin in March 2017, President Trump started a series of reforms to address the specific needs of veterans.

After hearing the concerns, in November 2017, President Trump approved H.R. 1329 / Public Law No. 115–75 Veterans' Compensation Cost-of-Living Adjustment Act of 2017, increasing the rates of veterans' wartime disability compensation, additional compensation for dependents, the clothing allowance for certain disabled veterans, and dependency and indemnity compensation for surviving spouses and children (sponsored by Representative Mike Bost, R-IL). Later in November, President Trump approved H.R. 3949 / Public Law No. 115–89 Veterans Apprenticeship and Labor Opportunity Reform Act (sponsored by Representative Ro Khanna, D-CA).

Through his personal generosity, President Trump supported the Veteran Administration by donating his first-quarter salary in 2018 to the Department of Veterans Affairs.

He continued to look out for veterans in 2018. On June 1, 2018, President Trump approved H.R. 3562 / Public Law No. 115–177 To amend title 38, United States Code, to authorize the Secretary of Veterans Affairs to furnish assistance for adaptations of residences of veterans in rehabilitation programs under chapter 31 of such title, and for other purposes. This allowed veterans up to $77,000 in assistance for residential adaptations in connection with service-related disabilities (sponsored by Representative Jodey C. Arrington, R-TX).

On June 6, 2018, President Trump approved S. 2372 / Public Law No. 115–182 John S. McCain III, Daniel K. Akaka, and Samuel R. Johnson VA Maintaining Internal Systems and Strengthening Integrated Outside Networks Act of 2018, the VA MISSION Act of 2018. This finally permitted veterans to seek hospital care, medical services, and extended care services to eligible veterans through non-Veteran Administration (VA) healthcare providers for real choice in healthcare (sponsored by Senator Johnny Isakson, R-GA).

In March 2019, President Trump signed Executive Order EO 13861-National Roadmap to Empower Veterans and End Suicide, known as the President's Roadmap to Empower Veterans and End a National Tragedy of Suicide, or

PREVENTS, establishing the Veteran Wellness, Empowerment, and Suicide Prevention Task Force.

Over the summer of 2019, President Trump approved H.R. 299 / Public Law No. 116–23 Blue Water Navy Vietnam Veterans Act of 2019 and S. 1749 / Public Law No. 116–33 Protecting Affordable Mortgages for Veterans Act of 2019, helping Vietnam veterans and mortgage-holding veterans, respectively.

In August 2019, President Trump signed Executive Order EO 13822-Supporting Our Veterans During Their Transition From Uniformed Service to Civilian Life, with the purpose of informing veterans transitioning into civilian life and improving mental healthcare, especially for those at high risk. Also in August, President Trump signed a Presidential Memorandum that discharged Federal student loan debt for totally and permanently disabled veterans.

In October 2019, President Trump signed Executive Order EO 13793-Improving Accountability and Whistleblower Protection at the Department of Veterans Affairs, in an effort to protect VA workers who are protecting veteran issues and fear retaliation.

Reason 15. The 1776 Project

On July 4, 2020, President Trump gave a message on America's 244th anniversary concerning the adoption of the Declaration of Independence. He acknowledged that when the Declaration was signed, America was young, eager, and finding its way by forming a new system of governance. He reminded Americans that the Founders knew there would be challenges to this form of governing, and that struggle would never end as the country grew in population. In 2020, Americans felt very real struggles, both in health and economic matters with the onslaught of COVID-19 and state-issued lockdowns, and from internal upheaval hijacked by covert groups ravaging large cities during injustice protests.

At Mount Rushmore, President Trump reminded Americans that the Founders, however wise they were, were also human, and flawed. Over time, America worked to remedy some of those flaws by fighting a bloody Civil War over the cause of slavery, and later, acknowledged more rights to Americans in the form of equality in voting, desegregation, and minority issues.

President Trump reminded that "western civilization and the triumph not only of spirit, but of wisdom, philosophy, and reason" were being threatened in 2020. He reminded that America has "a growing danger that threatens every blessing our ancestors fought so hard for, struggled, they bled to secure. Our nation is witnessing a merciless campaign to wipe out our history, defame our heroes, erase our values, and indoctrinate our children." He stated that this erroneous worldview of an inherently evil America was flawed, but was being promoted in education. He pointed out that "Those who seek to erase our heritage want Americans to forget our pride and our great dignity, so that we can no longer understand ourselves or America's destiny."

In September 2020, President Trump remarked at a White House Conference on American History, that in response to schools teaching distorted history, he would be signing an Executive Order to establish the 1776 Commission. The purpose of this was to promote patriotic education. He explained that the National Endowment for the Humanities awarded a grant to "support the development of a pro-American curriculum that celebrates the truth about our nation's great history." Scholars involved with the Commission include Professor Wilfred McClay, Dr. Peter Wood of the National Association of Scholars, and Ted Rebarber, CEO and founder of AccountabilityWorks.

President Trump continues to reach Americans about America's accomplishments, contributions, and future.

Reason 16. Standing Up to Socialism

President Trump affirms belief in America, confirming its foundation of using capitalism and self-driven meritorious work and the fruits that labor produces. He soundly opposes socialism, and denounces it publicly. At the State of the Union Address on February 6, 2019, he clearly stated, "Tonight, we renew our resolve that America will never be a socialist country." Later on February 4, 2020, he reiterated that with "Socialism destroys nations. But always remember: Freedom unifies the soul." He stoutly stands against flirting with seductive ideals like free college, free healthcare, free housing, free *everything*, and how allowing socialism, even democratic socialism, can lead to deeper problems citizens cannot vote their way out of.

Losing the control to vote for leadership leads to having no power to peacefully change leadership.

Reason 17. Calm in the Face of the Coronavirus Storm

During the first few months of the 2020 COVID-19 rush, President Trump and his task force of Dr. Anthony Fauci and Dr. Deborah Birx, headed by Vice President Mike Pence, appeared nearly daily before the public and press from the White House. These briefings outlined protocols, progress, national response, and professional outlook from both economic and medical views. President Trump's calm relaying of information prevented a full-on national panic, allowing Americans to function, think, and remain in control during this crisis rather than flat-out panic.

President Trump addressed some of the worst fears facing Americans, many out of school and working from home, or separated from a job entirely. In March 2020, national aid came in the form of immediate relief to tens of millions of student loan borrowers by suspending loan repayments and temporarily setting interest rates to 0 percent. This was later deferred until December 31, 2020, by President Trump signing a Memorandum on Continued Student Loan Payment Relief During the COVID-19 Pandemic.

President Trump also instructed the Internal Revenue Service to delay the requirement of the tax filing deadline and tax payment due for 2019, postponing filing and paying from April 15 to July 15, 2020.

To help Americans stay in their homes during this uncertain time, President Trump directed HUD and FHA to suspend foreclosures and evictions beginning in March 2020 for 60 days, and extended some dates several times as American jobs recovered. He also encouraged states and mortgage lenders to provide other forms of leniency, deferment, and payment delays for homeowners and renters.

Direct aid also came in the form of Federal extra unemployment amounts of $600 and stimulus checks to qualifying families and individuals through President Trump signing H.R.748 CARES Act. Also included was the Payment Protection Program for small businesses and subsidies for certain loan payments (with forgiveness for many).

As businesses opened up in May and more later in the summer, some states remained locked down to recovery. When Congress failed in responding with another citizen relief bill, President Trump signed a Memorandum on Deferring Payroll Tax Obligations in Light of the Ongoing COVID-19 Disaster, effectively suspending certain Federal tax obligations and allowing working Americans to bring home larger paychecks from September 1, 2020 through December 31, 2020 (for qualifying individuals), without penalties or additional taxes.

As New York City was overwhelmed with COVID-19 cases and hospitals faced potential shortages of ventilators, medical equipment, and bed space, Preside Trump responded to Governor Cuomo's pleas for aid. Help came in the form of USNS *Comfort*, one of two Navy Hospital Ships responding for service to lend medical facilities in the pandemic. The second hospital ship, the USNS *Mercy*, was designated to treat patients in Los Angeles. The *Comfort* was taken out of maintenance and put into emergency service in four days, destination Pier 90 New York City Harbor, in record time.

The U.S. Army Corps of Engineers and Federal Emergency Management Agency (FEMA) also set up a field hospital in New York's Javits Center with nearly 3,000 beds. Using commercial and private sectors, FEMA and Health and Human Services (HHS) supplied 11.6 million N95 respirators, 26 million surgical masks, 52 million face shields, 43 million surgical gowns, 22 million gloves, and 8,100 ventilators in record time. Cooperating with other countries, the Trump Administration secured medical supplies for the U.S. Project "Airbridge" that landed at JFK Airport with nearly two million masks and gowns, over 10 million gloves, and over 70,000 thermometers. Roughly 50 flights were expected. Once America's needs were met, with 100 days as an estimate, the U.S. would continue producing supplies, eventually stocking U.S. warehouses (left depleted by the previous administration) and resupplying the world's shelves.

While food runs on supermarkets emptied shelves of food, paper goods, and sanitizing products, private companies continued to retool to manufacture hand sanitizer, toilet tissue, and food. With American factories and businesses shut down and schools and eat-in restaurant dining rooms closed, farmers and ranchers were faced with the problem of livestock and produce surpluses. Produce rotted in the fields and on the vine, and livestock was unmoved to processing, backing up supply chains. This odd imbalance of surplus on the supply side and unavailability on store shelves created panic and chaos for shoppers, farmers, and ranchers.

In April 2020, President Trump and Secretary of Agriculture Sonny Perdue announced the $19 billion Coronavirus Food Assistance Program, created to supply fresh produce, dairy, and meat products to families in need. The USDA, under the Families First Coronavirus Response Act, purchased and distributed $3 billion of agricultural products, helping out farmers, ranchers, producers, and American families. Farmers to Families Food Box programs reached across the country, with multiple rounds following over the next few months, with a completion date of October 31, 2020.

On the medical front, President Trump tapped pharmaceutical companies and laboratories to create new, faster, and more accurate tests to be performed safely with the expertise from companies like Abbott, Cepheid, BD Veritor, and Quidel. By the end of July 2020, the U.S. was averaging 810,000 tests per day, with more than 930,000 COVID-19 tests conducted in one single day.

By addressing the food and medical security issues during the COVID-19 pandemic and other direct support, President Trump aided numerous sections of national recovery. These measures eased the unavoidable COVID-19 burden on millions of Americans as President Trump readied the country to return to full economic force.

Reason 18. Retooling Manufacturing for COVID-19 Emergency

When COVID-19 welled into a nationwide epidemic in early 2020, President Trump requested that America's companies step up production on essentials like respirators, medical supplies, and hospital equipment, as well as keep supermarket shelves stocked. American companies responded swiftly.

One new Phoenix factory opened in under five weeks, creating 500 new jobs, plus another 500 jobs in Rhode Island. These new factories combined would produce over 20 million N95 respirators every month. Hockey equipment manufacturer Bauer in New Hampshire switched to make face shields for medical staff, with 24 employees making 4,000 units per day. Under FEMA, HHS, and other private sector companies, over 70 million N95 respirators, 112 million surgical masks, seven million face shields, 18 million gowns, and nearly one billion gloves were manufactured to equip medical workers. Honeywell's Muskegon, Michigan, chemical manufacturing plant shifted operations to produce hand sanitizer. Companies like Brown-Forman and L'Oréal North America also switched manufacturing from luxury products to hand sanitizer.

Los Angeles-based Reformation mobilized local manufacturers to make five million face masks by converting its factory and using existing fabrics from its warehouse, focusing on the local homeless shelters. Nordstrom and Kaas Tailored in Washington, Oregon, Texas, California, New York, Illinois, New Jersey, Florida, and Washington, D.C. sewed nearly one million masks for Providence Health & Services and Ascension.

Ford partnered with 3M to produce medical equipment using its auto assembly lines after designing a "powered air-purifying respirator" (PAPR), allowing healthcare workers safety in contaminated environments. Outside Flat Rock, Michigan, paid UAW volunteers assembled the respirators at a Ford plant from modified auto parts from the Ford F-150 truck line. Output for these was quoted at 100,000 respirators or more. In Plymouth, a plant readied to produce three million face shields, and worked with supplier Joyson Safety Systems to manufacture airbag materials into reusable medical gowns, while producing face masks at its transmission plant.

General Motors joined Ventec to retool a Kokomo, Indiana, plant to produce ventilators. GM shipped 600 ventilators during April, and was ready to fill the federal government's 30,000 ventilators order by the end of August, if needed. GM retooled its Warren, Michigan, facility to produce face masks, with a capacity of 1.5 million masks a month.

Dow (chemicals) and SC Johnson converted one line of its largest manufacturing facility in Wisconsin and produced 75,000 bottles of hand sanitizer per month for frontline workers. Bacardi used eight of its distilleries to make ethanol (used in manufacturing hand sanitizer), producing more than 260,000 gallons of hand sanitizer to donate.

Brooks Brothers refit three U.S. factories (for shirts and ties) to produce surgical masks and medical gowns for frontline workers for up to 150,000 masks. Hanesbrands cut and sewed masks from its T-shirt three-ply jersey cotton, and along with other companies (Parkdale Inc., the U.S.'s largest yarn spinner, joining with Fruit of the Loom, American Giant, Los Angeles Apparel, AST Sportswear, Sanmar, America Knits, Beverly Knits, and Riegel Linen) produced over 300 million masks. In Chaska, Minnesota, MyPillow owner Mike Lindell dedicated 75 percent of his pillow-production facility to sewing cotton face masks for healthcare workers.

While most companies volunteered or responded quickly when asked to produce or retool to manufacture needed COVID-19 emergency supplies, President Trump did sign a Presidential Memorandum directing the Secretary of Health and Human Services to utilize all authority available under the Defense Production Act in March 2020.

The outpouring of President Trump's all-hands approach to combating COVID-19 unified some of America's most iconic brands to meet America's basic needs.

Reason 19. Operation Warp Speed to a COVID-19 Vaccine

With America holding its breath to ride out the COVID-19 restrictions, President Trump kick-started the search for a virus vaccine into high gear. By enlisting the expertise of major companies like Moderna, Sanofi, GlaxoSmithKline, and Johnson & Johnson, President Trump requested vaccine research to be taken to safe speeds, under revised FDA guidelines. He also turned to Corning and SiO2 Materials Science to increase production of vaccine delivery supplies like vials, needles and syringes. This cut down the time a vaccine could be in introduced to the public.

While research and testing was conducted, supply manufacturing and logistics were fine-tuned so the final tested and verified vaccines could reach the public quicker. This simultaneous approach put the warp speed in Operation Warp Speed. In response to the need for haste, the FDA authorized over 200 tests under emergency authorities by August 11, 2020, including nearly 170 molecular tests, nearly 40 antibody tests, and two antigen tests.

At the same time, President Trump requested rapid delivery of an effective vaccine, including manufacturing, to run in parallel to late stage clinical trials so that once a safe vaccine was formulated and passed testing, it could be distributed quickly to the public. In this way, there would be less lag in getting the vaccine out.

Reason 20. Law & Order

President Trump pushed to bring law and order to states, cities, and the surrounding countryside (even before protests and riots during the COVID-19 lockdowns and staggered state open ups). During January 2017, he signed Executive Order EO 13768-Enhancing Public Safety in the Interior of the United States, Executive Order EO 13769-Protecting the Nation From Foreign Terrorist Entry Into the United States, and Executive Order EO 13863-Taking Additional Steps to Address the National Emergency With Respect to Significant Transnational Criminal Organizations (this amended EO 13581, July 24, 2011).

In May 2019, President Trump approved H.R. 2379 / Public Law No. 116–18 To reauthorize the Bulletproof Vest Partnership Grant Program, which gave permanent authority for the Bulletproof Vest Partnership (BVP) Program. This provided grants to states and localities for the purchase of body armor vests for law enforcement officers, and renamed the program the Patrick Leahy Bulletproof Vest Partnership Grant Program. (Sponsored by Representative Bill Pascrell, Jr., D-NJ.)

In 2017, President Trump also approved Executive Order EO 13776-Task Force on Crime Reduction and Public Safety and signed H.R. 3249 / Public Law No. 115–185 Project Safe Neighborhoods Grant Program Authorization Act of 2018, and began removing violent gang members, criminals, and predators from U.S. communities. Project Safe Neighborhoods worked with the Department of Justice (DOJ) to create safer neighborhoods through continued crime reduction in several areas (sponsored by Representative Barbara Comstock, R-VA), vital to later violence tearing some of America's largest cities apart as business tried to open after the COVID-19 lockdown. After two deaths from protest/riots in Kenosha, Wisconsin, in

August 2020, President Trump sent in federal troops to aid the city in protecting itself from the violence.

President Trump further protected American history and significant sites by signing Executive Order 13933-Protecting American Monuments, Memorials, and Statues and Combating Recent Criminal Violence in June 2020. In response to the protest/riots plaguing some cities during the COVID-19 lockdowns in 2020, President Trump announced the Department of Justice would provide more than $61 million in grants to hire hundreds of new city police officers for Operation LeGend, named for a four-year-old Missouri boy who was shot during the surge in violence. Witnessing some mayors of these large cities allow unchecked anarchy in their cities, President Trump offered to send in federal troops (as in Kenosha), and signed a Memorandum on Reviewing Funding to State and Local Government Recipients That Are Permitting Anarchy, Violence, and Destruction in American Cities.

President Trump also denounced crime groups. On September 14, 2017, in response to an outbreak of violence in Charlottesville, Virginia, President Trump approved S.J. Res. 49 / Public Law No. 115–58, condemning the violence and domestic terrorist attack that took place during events between August 11 and August 12, 2017, in Charlottesville, Virginia. This recognized the first responders who lost their lives while monitoring the events, offered condolences to the families and friends of those individuals who were killed and understanding and support to individuals injured by the violence, while expressing support for the Charlottesville community. Through the signing, President Trump also rejected White nationalists, White supremacists, the Ku Klux Klan, neo-Nazis, and other hate groups. The Law also urged the President and the President's Cabinet to use all available resources to address the threats posed by those groups.

President Trump empowered survivors of sexual violence in September 2018, when he approved S. 717 / Public Law No.

115–237 Pro bono Work to Empower and Represent Act of 2018. This required each judicial district chief justice to hold public events promoting pro bono legal services for survivors of domestic violence, dating violence, sexual assault, and stalking, plus hold additional public events for Indian or Alaska Native victims if the district included such persons (sponsored by Senator Dan Sullivan, R-AK). He also approved S. 2961 / Public Law No. 115–424 Victims of Child Abuse Act Reauthorization Act of 2018.

As America slowly got to its feet after the COVID-19 lockdowns, President Trump supported law and order, and the safety of Americans and businesses in their own cities

Reason 21. U.S. Pipelines

President Trump understood America's great resources, and promised while campaigning to tap into that vast energy using innovative as well as proven methods. To get the U.S. out from under problematic foreign energy dependency, President Trump signed the Presidential Memorandum Regarding Construction of American Pipelines, the Presidential Memorandum Regarding Construction of the Keystone XL Pipeline, and the Presidential Memorandum Regarding Construction of the Dakota Access Pipeline in January 2017. In July 2020, President Trump signed several Presidential Permits, allowing operation of the Burgos pipeline project and the Nuevo Laredo project.

These far-reaching pipelines allowed Keystone XL and Dakota Access pipelines to continue construction, creating an estimated 42,000 jobs and $2 billion in economic benefits, heavily contributing to America's energy independence.

Reason 22. Supporting Historically Black Colleges and Universities

In February 2017, President Trump held a listening session attended by Historically Black Colleges and Universities (HBCU) leaders. Among them were representatives from Thurgood Marshall College Fund, United Negro College Fund, and National Association for Equal Opportunity in Higher Education, as well as Education Secretary Betsy DeVos.

Later in February, after listening to HBCU concerns, President Trump signed Executive Order EO 13779-White House Initiative To Promote Excellence and Innovation at Historically Black Colleges and Universities announcing the President's Board of Advisors on HBCU. He placed Johnny Taylor, Jr., former seven-year president of the Thurgood Marshall College fund, as Chairman of the President's Board of Advisors on Historically Black Colleges and Universities. President Trump also called for millions of dollars more in funding and a $400 million increase for Federal TRiO Programs and a $300 million increase for Federal Work Study.

President Trump signed a farm bill of over $100 million in scholarships, research, and centers of excellence for HBCU land-grant institutions. He also forgave Hurricane Katrina disaster loans for Dillard University, Southern University at New Orleans, Tougaloo College, and Xavier University of Louisiana so the schools could focus on educating and looking to the future. He prompted Congress to pass a permanent $255 million in annual funding to HBCU in December 2019.

Reason 23. Jobs, Jobs, Jobs

In February 2017, President Trump held a listening session with retail industry leaders representing many areas in the job market. Among them were Jill Soltau with JoAnn Fabric and

Craft Stores, Art Peck with The Gap, Bill Rhodes with AutoZone, Hubert Joly with Best Buy, Brian Cornell with Target, Stefano Pessina of Walgreens Boots Alliance, Marvin Ellison with J.C. Penney, and Greg Sandfort with Tractor Supply Company.

With President Trump taking office, retailers knew they had a better future selling front. Wal-Mart planned to add 10,000 U.S. jobs in 2017, and Amazon another 100,000 fulltime U.S. jobs over the next eighteen months. President-Elect Trump also met with Carrier Corp. to keep 1,000 jobs in Indiana. Ford rerouted a planned Mexico plant to Flat Rock, Michigan, adding 700 U.S. jobs and $700 million in investment. President-Elect Trump put his deal-making skills to use in negotiating deals with Lockheed Martin Corp., which lowered the cost of producing the F-35 fighter plane and added another 1,800 workers to a Texas plant to build them.

Jobs did come back to the U.S. With President Trump at the discussion table in 2018, Nikola Motor Company chose Buckeye, Arizona, to build a new hydrogen-electric semi-truck manufacturing headquarters, including a one million square-foot building west of Phoenix. Fiat Chrysler Automobiles (FCA) made good on its announcement a year ago and moved its Ram heavy-duty pickup truck to a Warren, Michigan, plant from Mexico. This added 2,500 jobs to the Warren plant.

In March 2018, U.S. Steel announced it would reopen steelmaking facilities and restart one of two blast furnaces at its Granite City, Illinois, plant. This required 500 new employees. Officials for the company cited President Trump's tariffs on steel and aluminum imports as a pivotal factor.

Of the 312,000 new jobs in December 2018, the most gains came in healthcare (50,000), food and drinking (41,000), construction (38,000), and manufacturing (32,000). By comparison, December of 2013 saw healthcare lose 6,000 jobs, food and drinking gained 12,000, construction lost 16,000, and manufacturing added 9,000 (for a total gain of 74,000 jobs that month).

Under President Trump's direction, American jobs came back, expanded, and created a new, booming economy.

Reason 24. Apprenticeships & Vocational Education

In June of 2017, President Trump promoted a time-honored pathway for non-college students to enter the workforce with good-paying, stable jobs. Many jobs like machinists, skilled trades, and journeymen were falling away as jobs left America for cheaper labor and fewer regulations in other countries. Meanwhile, the aging workforce with that hands-on knowledge was retiring, with few younger workers taking their place. America was one generation away from losing these skilled workers, many from apprenticeships in the 1970 and 1980s job force.

President Trump recognized this as he signed Executive Order 13801-Expanding Apprenticeships in America, on June 15, 2017. This was a much-needed program nationwide as the demand for non-college trade and mechanical jobs soared under the Trump Administration. "Apprenticeships place students into great jobs without the crippling debt of traditional four-year college degrees," President Trump stated at the signing. "Instead, apprentices earn while they learn."

No standard college was needed for good, steady, and well-paying jobs, a path many new high school graduates welcomed. By November 2018, the Trump Administration had addressed the need for new skilled workers for manufacturing and construction jobs with apprenticeships and mentoring. Vocational and trade schools become more popular—and the need for them was escalating as the economy grew. Students who once looked at spending upwards of $125,000 for a

Bachelor's degree were now looking earnestly at investing around \$33,000 for specialized training in a variety of vocational/trade schools, or earning as they learned in an apprenticeship. This more custom-fit training appealed to many students not interested in traditional college education. Blue-collar workers suddenly had salaries out-pacing white-collar sectors, also appealing to many new workers. Revitalization of the need for less-college educated workers ramped up after President Trump signed the GOP tax bill in 2017, bringing less regulation in many manufacturing areas and tax-cuts to businesses.

In the summer of 2018, Congress' bipartisan effort reauthorized the Carl D. Perkins Career and Technical Education Act, which had been untouched for 12 years. President Trump signed Public Law No. 115-224 Strengthening Career and Technical Education for the 21st Century Act, which reauthorized the Carl D. Perkins Career and Technical Education Act of 2006 through FY2024. (Sponsored by Representative Glenn Thompson, R-PA.)

President Trump ushered in more winning in the workplace. President Trump signed Executive Order EO 13845-Establishing the President's National Council for the American Worker. Faced with a skills crisis since employment had boomed in 2018, President Trump addressed the need for America's students and workers to have access to affordable, relevant, and innovative education and job training to equip them to compete and win in the global economy. When President Trump approved the above mentioned Law (H.R. 2353 / Public Law No. 115–224), included was a requirement for states to reserve funds to recruit special populations (those from economically challenged families) for enrollment into career and technical education (CTE) programs.

Since January 2017, over 500,000 people had entered apprenticeship programs registered with the Department of Labor or state counterparts, with an average starting salary (for those having completed apprenticeships) exceeding $70,000 (2019 statistics).

Skilled workers were back in demand. After a manufacturing lull of the workforce, companies reported that finding qualified industrial manufacturing personnel was the biggest issue for the next few years. The need for skilled tool and die, mechanics, electricians, and the need to find young people entering and completing apprenticeships were their (company's) largest concerns, according to September 2017's Manufacturers' Outlook Survey from the National Association of Manufacturers.

By 2018, in the first quarter Outlook Survey by NAM, manufacturers reported more difficulty filling jobs with qualified workers. Over 70 percent stated they would be interested in participating in the apprenticeship programs the Trump Administration promoted. When asked what they found most challenging in the coming months, survey respondents listed "immigration policies", "hiring qualified personnel", "intellectual property protection", and the coming "2018 election". These comments came from manufacturers in machinery, fabricated metal products, primary metals, and specialty manufacturing.

Motor City revival of 2018. To help meet the demand for hands-on jobs, Detroit high school students took part in pre-apprenticeship programs, and were able to work with construction and other companies. These were part of the growing demand in blue-collar jobs, an estimated 7.2 million jobs, the most since 2008 (with the lowest being January 2011, with 5,427,000).

President Trump continues to look for ways to bring more jobs to Americans with fair trade dealings.

Reason 25. Defense & Military Build Up

On July 20, 2017, President Trump signed Executive Order EO 13806-Assessing and Strengthening the Manufacturing and Defense Industrial Base and Supply Chain Resiliency of the United States. This was the start of President Trump rebuilding the U.S. military and defense regards, which were in dire need of reconstruction.

In August 2018, President Trump signed the $717 billion FY2019 National Defense Authorization Act, this time including a pay raise for over 15,000 active duty service members. In December 2019, President Trump signed the National Defense Authorization Act (NDAA) for FY2020, authorizing the historical amount of $738 billion in defense spending. These two authorizations allowed military interests and defense areas to bulk up dwindling protections, including 77 F-35 joint strike fighters, F-35 spares, development of the B-21 bomber, shipbuilding for 13 new battle force ships, funding acceleration for future ships, three Arleigh Burke-class destroyers, two Virginia-class submarines, three littoral combat ships, 24 F/A-18 Super Hornets, ten P-8A Poseidons, two KC-130J Hercules, 25 AH-1Z Cobras, seven MV-22/CMV-22B Ospreys, and three MQ-4 Tritons. Funding also went toward training and equipping Iraqi security forces to counter Islamic State of Iraq and Syria (ISIS) terrorists and accelerated research in hyperspace technology and defense against hyperspace missiles, as well as developmental funding for artificial intelligence capabilities.

While beefing up the military air power, President-Elect Trump also put his deal-making skills to use in negotiating with Lockheed Martin Corp., which lowered the cost of producing those F-35 fighters (built in Texas).

President Trump believes in a strong military, but as he added on September 10, 2020, at a press briefing (and many other times), "We have the newest, best military we've ever had. So, hopefully, we won't have to use it."

Reason 26. Getting the U.S. out of NAFTA

In mid-August 2017, President Trump began renegotiating NAFTA with Canada and Mexico for better terms for the U.S.'s interests. He wanted more (at least 75 percent) of automobile parts to be made in the U.S., Canada or Mexico. He wanted better markets for U.S. dairy and wine producers, higher standards for trucks crossing the U.S.-Mexico border, better protection for patents and intellectual properties, more protection for U.S. drugs against generics in Mexico and Canada (ten years rather than five and eight), and better dispute resolution. These changes would later become the United States-Mexico-Canada Agreement (USMCA) in 2020, which President Trump signed on November 30, 2018 (along with Mexican President Enrique Peña Nieto and Canadian Prime Minister Justin Trudeau).

The House of Representatives passed the bill in December 2019. The USMCA entered into force on July 1, 2020. President Trump got his better deal for U.S. workers.

Reason 27. Record Breaking Employment

Economic factors began to take shape as soon as President Trump took office. By the end of January 2017, the civilian unemployment rate, seasonally adjusted for January 2017, was at 4.8 overall, with Black or African American at 7.8, Latino or Hispanic at 5.9, Asian at 3.8, and White at 4.3. In January 2017, nonfarm payroll increased by 227,000 in the U.S. Most came from retail, construction, financial entities, bar and restaurant, and professional and technical services, followed by healthcare additions. North Dakota led the lowest unemployment rate with 2.6.

Numerous states reached new unemployment lows in early 2017. The unemployment rate in Arkansas set a new low in February at 3.7 percent (previously 4.1) and Oregon set a new low at 4.0 percent, down from the previous 5.1 (since 1976). By the end of March 2017, the civilian unemployment rate, seasonally adjusted for March 2017, was at 4.5 overall. Professional and business services had the greatest gains, while mining followed, adding 11,000 jobs. Unemployment finished lower in March 2017 than 2016 in 336 of 388 metropolitan areas. Leading these states were the cities of Ocean City, New Jersey, and Grand Junction, Colorado, with 74 others reporting declines of at least a 1.0 percentage point. In April 2017, nonfarm payroll gained 211,000 in the U.S. The employment-to-population ratio grew to 60.2 percent, the highest level since February 2009. Jobs added came in leisure and hospitality (55,000 added), healthcare, social assistance, financial, professional and business services, and mining. The number of total nonfarm job openings rose to 6.0 million in April 2017, the highest on record (since Bureau of Labor Statistics (BLS) records from 2007).

The total nonfarm job openings rose to 6.2 million in June 2017, a ten-year high. At the close of 2017, the civilian unemployment rate, seasonally adjusted for December 2017, was at 4.1 overall, with Black or African American at 6.8 (the lowest ever to that date), Latino or Hispanic at 4.9, Asian at 2.5, and White at 3.7.

American jobs flooded back with President Trump's changes in restrictive business red tape and regulations from the top down to local businesses. In March of 2018, the U.S. jobs market set a *seventeen-year record high* in demand for workers, a surge that started the previous January.

April 2018 ended with great employment numbers as California, Hawaii, and Wisconsin set new unemployment lows. The civilian unemployment rate, seasonally adjusted for April 2018, was at 3.9 overall, with Black or African American at 6.6, Latino or Hispanic at 4.8, Asian at 2.8, and White at 3.6. In April 2018, jobs in manufacturing, metal fabricating, machinery, and healthcare made the most gains. Jobless rates in California (4.2 percent), Hawaii (2.0 percent), and Wisconsin (2.8 percent) set new lows, since 1976. A total of 16 states had unemployment rates much lower than the U.S. average of 3.9 percent.

As July 2018 rolled in, U.S. employment was at full charge. With the rampant growth in business over the last eighteen months, some companies scrambled to find qualified workers. An aging workforce in journeyman and skilled trades and little demand for new workers over the pre-2016 years left large voids in the rising demand. The Trump Administration initiated apprenticeship programs to fill this gap. Also, the influx of allotted funds for jobs in infrastructure increased what had been a dwindling call for construction workers. By the last business day of July 2018, job openings were at 6,939,000, the *highest level on record* for BLS.

Record-setting job creation continued through August 2018. Average hourly earnings increased by 77 cents, or 2.9 percent, over the year, for an average of $27.16. Hawaii had the lowest unemployment rate at 2.1 percent in August. Rates in Idaho (2.8 percent), Oregon (3.8 percent), South Carolina (3.4 percent), and Washington (4.5 percent) *set record lows* (since record keeping began in 1976). Iowa set a high bar in October 2018 with 1.1 unemployment.

December 2018 registered Black or African American unemployment at 6.6 (lowest ever to that date), with Latino or Hispanic at 4.4, Asian at 3.3, and White at 3.4. By August 2019, Black or African American employment would *hit an all-time low* of 5.4 and stay at 6.0 or below until the COVID-19 pandemic in 2020. Hispanic or Latino unemployment would drop to the *lowest level ever* of 3.9 in September 2019 and remain under 4.4 until the COVID-19 panic.

Overall unemployment was at 3.5 in February 2020, the lowest in 50 years, until COVID-19 took over within a few weeks. With President Trump protecting American workers and companies, the U.S. workforce can reach that level again.

Reason 28. Bringing Back Mining

Coal and mining jobs had fallen into nearly unrecoverable slumps during the last six years before President Trump took office. Some politicians even applauded these job losses.

In March 2017, coal mining returned to Kentucky after President Trump overturned Obama Administration regulations that shuttered the coal industry, forcing 460 workers to be laid-off in 2012 in the Perry County mine alone. The steady decline of coal industry jobs and closed mines ravaged coal country in the U.S. Over 80,000 jobs were gone, promised to never return due to President Obama's pledge to "bankrupt" the industry. The Obama Administration's Environmental Protection Agency (EPA) practices saw to the closing or bankruptcy of large coal companies like Peabody Energy Corp, the U.S.'s largest coal miner, and Arch Coal and Alliance Coal.

In early April 2017, as President Trump lifted coal mining restrictions and overturned the EPA regulations (assessed and then later replaced with the Affordable Clean Energy (ACE) rule), Peabody Energy Corp returned after bankruptcy and plant closings, as did other mines. Coal miners went back to work by the thousands.

By the end of March 2017, the civilian unemployment rate, seasonally adjusted for March 2017, was at 4.5 overall. This was important to the mining industry because after professional and business services (with the greatest gains), mining followed, adding 11,000 jobs. By mid-July 2017, U.S. mining and logging jobs had grown by 42,000 since January 2017. Through 2019, coal exports had beaten the 2017 Energy Information Administration (EIA) forecasts by more than 54 percent since President Trump took office.

In addition, the Trump Administration had accelerated development of alternative uses of coal, such as coal-to-products and coal-based hydrogen production that offered new markets for coal. President Trump remains a strong supporter of carbon capture and storage (CCS) technologies, critical to fossil energy and many industrial processes, with the 45Q tax credits in the Bipartisan Budget Act of 2018 and the recently proposed guidance from the IRS.

Effective September 2019, the Clean Power Plan was repealed and replaced with the Affordable Clean Energy rule. As one senator put it earlier in an August 2018 White House statement, ". . . the EPA's newly proposed Affordable Clean Energy plan allows state input and clearly signals the War on Coal is over."

Reason 29. U.S. Embassy Moves to Jerusalem

In the first week of December 2017, President Trump signed Proclamation 9683-Recognizing Jerusalem as the Capital of the State of Israel and Relocating the United States Embassy to Israel to Jerusalem. This was a step toward physically relocating the U.S. Embassy in Israel from Tel Aviv to Jerusalem, something Congress had urged since the Jerusalem Embassy Act of 1995 (Public Law 104-45).

In May 2018, the United States Embassy officially opened in Jerusalem, coinciding with the 70th anniversary of the Israeli Declaration of Independence.

With this, President Trump set the stage to barter peace in the Middle East later, bringing centuries-long enemies to a peace signing agreement.

Reason 30. ISIS Defeated

In January 2017, President Trump set forth a Memorandum on the Plan To Defeat the Islamic State of Iraq and Syria. By December 2017, the Iraqi government announced all Iraqi territory taken by ISIS had been liberated from ISIS control.

Going into 2018, the Trump Administration continued to work with the Global Coalition, Iraqi Security Forces, and Syrian Democratic Forces to destroy ISIS and liberate territories taken by the self-declared caliphate.

In October 2019, President Trump announced that U.S. forces had killed Abu Bakr al-Baghdadi, the founder and leader of ISIS, in a successful and precise raid. On January 3, 2020, Iranian Islamic Revolutionary Guard Corps and Quds Force commander general Qasem Soleimani was killed by U.S. military in another exact strike, taking out the world's number one terrorist.

Without exasperating further war in the Middle East, President Trump had enabled U.S. forces and military allies to remove two notorious terrorist leaders.

Reason 31. Prescription Drug Reform

President Trump looks out for healthcare costs. In October 2018, President Trump approved S. 2553 / Public Law No. 115–262 Know the Lowest Price Act of 2018, and approved S. 2554 / Public Law No. 115–263 Patient Right to Know Drug

Prices Act. These acted in the recipient's (we, the patient or consumer) best interest to allow Medicare or Medicare Advantage users to know the differences between costs covered, out-of-pocket costs, and even lower costs for non-insurance paying, and addressed antitrust filing requirements in the Medicare Prescription Drug, Improvement, and Modernization Act of 2003. (S. 2553 was sponsored by Senator Debbie Stabenow, D-MI, and S. 2554 was sponsored by Senator Susan M. Collins, R-ME.)

In July 2020, President Trump signed Executive Order EO 13939-Lowering Prices for Patients by Eliminating Kickbacks to Middlemen, which directs discounts and rebates offered on prescription drugs to be passed on to patients instead of middlemen.

President Trump also addressed the rising cost of insulin, instructing the Centers for Medicare and Medicaid Services (CMS) ensure that Medicare beneficiary prescription drug plans cap the costs of insulin at $35 in out-of-pocket expenses for a 30-day supply.

Reason 32. The Opioid Crisis

In March 2017, President Trump held a listening session on opioid and drug abuse. It was attended by Governor Chris Christie, Secretary of the VA David Shulkin, Secretary of Education Betsy DeVos, Don Wright (Acting Assistant Secretary for Health), Richard Baum (Acting Director of the Office of National Drug Control Policy), Bertha Madras of Harvard Medical School, and family members of those affected by drugs and opioid abuse, to listen to their stories, experiences, and advice. On April 3, 2017, President Trump signed Executive Order EO 13784-Establishing the President's Commission on Combating Drug Addiction and the Opioid

Crisis, allowing the study and actions to remedy the drug issues.

This was followed in June 2018 by the Youth Opioid Prevention Ad Campaign to address the opioid problems plaguing adults age 18-24. In late October 2018, President Trump approved H.R. 6 / Public Law No. 115–271 Substance Use-Disorder Prevention that Promotes Opioid Recovery and Treatment for Patients and Communities Act. This enabled better care for those faced with opioid challenges by prohibiting termination of Medicaid eligibility for juveniles while being inmates at public institutions, established drug-review, use requirements and safety measures for new opioid prescriptions, and made state Medicaid programs cover residential pediatric recovery services for infants with neonatal abstinence syndrome. (Sponsored by Representative Greg Walden, R-OR.)

President Trump continues to battle the opioid crisis in his September 2020 Executive Order in the America-First Healthcare Plan.

Reason 33. The Right to Try

On May 30, 2018, President Trump approved S. 204 / Public Law No. 115–176 Trickett Wendler, Frank Mongiello, Jordan McLinn, and Matthew Bellina Right to Try Act of 2017. This promoted a patient's rights to allow terminally ill patients to voluntarily choose a medication not yet FDA approved, freeing up patient options otherwise unavailable to them (sponsored by Senator Ron Johnson, R-WI).

Reason 34. Healthcare and Preexisting Conditions

In February 2017, President Trump held a listening session with health insurance company CEOs to get their input and help determine how best to improve healthcare for U.S. citizens. Later in October, President Trump signed Executive Order EO 13813-Promoting Healthcare Choice and Competition Across the United States, freeing up choice for patients.

In 2019, he followed by signing Executive Order EO 13877-Improving Price and Quality Transparency in American Healthcare To Put Patients First. This affected EO 13813, October 12, 2017. He also signed Executive Order EO 13879-Advancing American Kidney Health.

As new healthcare measures are taken, President Trump continues to assure the American public that preexisting conditions inclusions must be part of any new healthcare issues. He reiterated this in a Fox News Town Hall in Scranton, PA, on March 6, 2020, stating preexisting conditions were 100 percent protected in the new healthcare plan. This turned into President Trump signing an Executive Order on the America-First Healthcare Plan, covering the implementation of Executive Order EO 13937 Access to Affordable Life-Saving Medications and other signings in September 2020.

The America-First Healthcare Plan expands health savings accounts (HSA), makes permanent many of the new policies outlined in Improving Rural Health and Telehealth Access (Executive Order 13941), including accessibility and availability of telehealth services (and healthcare infrastructure) for rural Americans, lowers cost for insulin and injectable epinephrine for lower-income Americans (Executive Order 13937), and repealed the medical device tax.

President Trump wants a healthcare plan for American that has a "steadfast commitment to always protecting individuals with pre-existing conditions and ensuring they have access to the high-quality healthcare they deserve".

Reason 35. Border Control & Immigration

Candidate Donald Trump ran his 2016 presidential campaign on strengthening U.S. borders and the laws on illegal immigration. This continued to be a focus once he took residence in the White House. In the first few weeks of taking office in January 2017, President Trump signed Executive Order EO 13767-Border Security and Immigration Enforcement Improvements, including the Immigration and Nationality Act (INA), the Secure Fence Act of 2006 (Public Law 109-367) (Secure Fence Act), and the Illegal Immigration Reform and Immigrant Responsibility Act of 1996 (Public Law 104-208 Div. C) (IIRIRA). This outlined President Trump's plans for a physical wall along the U.S.-Mexico border where feasible and needed, operational measures to control contraband, drugs, gang travel, and terrorism, and points of entry.

In April of 2017, President Trump signed Memorandum Implementing Immediate Heightened Screening and Vetting of Applications for Visas and Other Immigration Benefits, Ensuring Enforcement of All Laws for Entry Into the United States, and Increasing Transparency Among Departments and Agencies of the Federal Government and for the American People. This helped protect U.S. citizens, and was followed on September 24, 2017, when President Trump signed Proclamation 9645-Enhancing Vetting Capabilities and Processes for Detecting Attempted Entry Into the United States by Terrorists or Other Public-Safety Threats. There were 310,531 illegal alien border-crossing apprehensions nationwide in 2017 (fiscal year). Of the illegal aliens arrested by

Immigration and Customs Enforcement (ICE), more than 92 percent had criminal convictions or pending criminal charges, were ICE fugitives, or were illegal reentrants.

In February 2018, President Trump held a roundtable discussion on violent gang and MS-13 activity, including input with Homeland Security, the Attorney General's office, U.S. Immigration and Customs Enforcement Special Agent in Charge, and several Representatives, among others. Topics included combating gang violence, illegal immigration, government shutdown over Deferred Action for Childhood Arrivals (DACA), more stringent border security measures, and criminal deportation. That April, President Trump signed a Presidential Memorandum for the Secretary of Defense, the Attorney General, the Secretary of Homeland Security regarding Securing the Southern Border of the United States, effectively ending the "catch and release" policy along the U.S.-Mexico border in April 2018.

In June 2018, President Trump signed Executive Order EO 13841-Affording Congress an Opportunity To Address Family Separation, to help address the growing number of "caravans" of illegal immigrants flooding the U.S.-Mexico border. With the expanding caravan populations and increase in organization, violence pervading the movement, and disregard for laws of and assimilation into existing citizenry, the deluge of illegal immigration taxed both Mexico and U.S. systems.

According to a November 2018 DHS release, of the large mass of immigrants trying to enter the U.S. illegally via the U.S. Southwest border (caravans), many migrants were from Central America. However, DHS also noted persons from Somalia, India, Haiti, Afghanistan, and Bangladesh in the caravan. After study, DHS found over 270 known criminals among the caravan. Discovery at the time showed more caravans were forming and expected over the next weeks and months. What began as a 2016 presidential election position turned into a challenge for political parties heading into the 2018 midterms and the 2020 presidential election.

In November 2018, President Trump signed Proclamation 9822-Addressing Mass Migration Through the Southern Border of the United States. This reinforced using existing laws regarding the massive amounts of illegal aliens crossing into the U.S. through Mexico from Central America, with sometimes up to 2,000 inadmissible aliens crossing into the U.S. daily.

President Trump found an ally with the election of President Andrés Manuel López Obrador as Mexico's new president in late 2018. With U.S.-Mexico cooperation, caravans were detained in Mexico rather than shown an open door into the United States. Using already existing aid from the U.S. in the amount of $10 billion, Mexico stepped up.

The Trump Administration used current U.S. laws to keep genuine asylum seekers at the border while their claims and circumstances were processed and investigated. Using 8 U.S. Code § 1158 - Asylum (United States Code, 2012 Edition, Supplement 3, Title 8 - ALIENS AND NATIONALITY), effective 2016, that required asylum seekers to request asylum in the first "Safe Third Country" they encountered—not necessarily the country they desired as destination, many caravan immigrants coming from Honduras, Guatemala and El Salvador through Mexico had to seek help from Mexico first.

Addressing migrant families at the border. In early January 2019, President Trump sent a Letter to Congress on Border Security. Included in the letter was the topic of terminating the *Flores* Settlement Agreement, which prevented families from being held together through removal and amending the Trafficking Victims Protection Reauthorization Act (TVPRA), to allow for the safe and humane return of illegally-smuggled minors back to their families in their home countries.

(The *Flores* Settlement Agreement resulted from a 1985 class action lawsuit against Immigration and Naturalization Service over the detention of minors. In 1988, President Nixon-appointed Judge Robert Kelleher of the U.S. District Court for the Central District of California ruled in favor of the groups bringing the case, but the case was reversed by three members of the Ninth Circuit Court of Appeals in 1990. A year later, the full eleven-judge court reversed their ruling and Judge Kelleher's rule stood. In 1992, the Supreme Court heard oral arguments in the case and a year later delivered a win to the government, voting 7-2 to reverse the lower court decision. Activists for the cause kept up pressure, and in 1997, the *Flores* Agreement was passed. This was followed by Congress passing the Trafficking Victims Protection Reauthorization Act, codifying parts of *Flores* into federal law in 2008. In 2015, President Obama-appointed California U.S. District Court Judge Dolly Gee expanded the "unaccompanied" aspect to include "accompanied children" and "without unnecessary delay" to mean twenty days. This set up the child separation issues at border detention for years.)

In July 2019, President Trump approved H.R. 3401 / Public Law No. 116–26 Emergency Supplemental Appropriations for Humanitarian Assistance and Security at the Southern Border Act, 2019. To halt future caravans, President Trump dealt with the countries of origin directly. From May through September 2019, President Trump made border security arrangements with Guatemala, El Salvador, and Honduras. In July 2019, President Trump signed the Safe Third Country Agreement with Guatemala, providing better cooperation with the U.S. and Guatemala in immigration issues.

President Trump continues to work on immigration issues, including chain migration, promoting merit-based immigration, and suspending visa lotteries.

Reason 36. U.S. Medicine Security

President Trump secures America's essential needs. Shortly after the presidential election of 2016, the U.S. business world began to look different, even before Donald Trump officially took the helm. One of these changes was Bayer AG, which, after meeting with President Trump, stated it would create thousands of jobs in the U.S. Bayer AG also stated it would put $8 billion in agricultural research into the U.S. over the next six years.

The directors of Civica and Medicines for All were part of a group of industry leaders raising the alarm about pharmaceutical supply chain vulnerabilities in 2018, and met with lawmakers in Washington, DC, to discuss possible solutions to providing medicine in the U.S. This was years before COVID-19.

After the brunt of the COVID-19 outbreak of 2020, President Trump signed Executive Order EO 13944-Ensuring Essential Medicines, Medical Countermeasures, and Critical Inputs Are Made in the United States in August 2020, to increase American production of essential medical supplies to lessen reliance on medicines from foreign sources. He also announced, "We must never be reliant on a foreign nation for America's medical or other needs." This directed the Commissioner of Food and Drugs to create a list of essential medicines, medical countermeasures, and other critical needs for the American public health. The Executive Order also accelerated domestic manufacturing of these essentials to ensure future demands and support production of advanced pharmaceutical ingredients and essential medicines in America. Agencies were allowed to prioritize permitting and approvals for domestic manufacturers.

Since 2000, most of the U.S.'s pharmaceutical drugs and generics came from offshore, namely China and India, putting

America at the mercy of possible political shifts or when shortages occurred that reduced exports. The U.S.'s reliance on vital medicines hampered national security. In response to COVID-19, President Trump continued to bring home medical needs by tapping companies like Phlow Corp., AMPAC Fine Chemicals, Amgen, Genentech, Gilead, Regeneron, and Civica based in the U.S. This had bipartisan support from Senator Marco Rubio (R-FL), Senator Elizabeth Warren (D-MA), Senator Kevin Cramer (R-ND), Senator Chris Murphy (D-CT), Senator Tim Kaine (D-VA), and Representative Michael Waltz (R-FL).

Reason 37. U.S. Food and Water Security

With uncanny foresight, President Trump approved H.R. 1238 / Public Law No. 115–43 Securing our Agriculture and Food Act in 2017 to maintain U.S. food and water reliability. In October 2018, President Trump approved S. 2269 / Public Law No. 115–266 Global Food Security Reauthorization Act of 2017 and a Presidential Memorandum on Promoting the Reliable Supply and Delivery of Water in the West in mid-October 2018. While these seemed like mundane signings, as the next few years wore on, COVID-19 taxed these reserves.

"The loss of more than 60,000 American factories, key companies, and almost 5 million manufacturing jobs since 2000 threatens to undermine the capacity and capabilities of United States manufacturers to meet national defense requirements and raises concerns about the health of the manufacturing and defense industrial base. The loss of additional companies, factories, or elements of supply chains could impair domestic capacity to create, maintain, protect, expand, or restore capabilities essential for national security," President Trump stated when signing Executive Order 13806 in July 2017 (Assessing and Strengthening the Manufacturing and

58

Defense Industrial Base and Supply Chain Resiliency of the United State).

These measures by President Trump, and the help of U.S. companies, stocked America's cupboards for future emergencies.

Reason 38. American Supply Chain Independence

In order to establish more self-reliance on American sources, President Trump signed Executive Order EO 13817-A Federal Strategy To Ensure Secure and Reliable Supplies of Critical Minerals, in December 2017. This readiness Executive Order included a list of crucial minerals like aluminum (bauxite), antimony, bismuth, cesium (photoelectric cell use), gallium (electronic circuits, semiconductors, pharmaceuticals, nuclear medicine tests), helium, lithium, magnesium, manganese, niobium, platinum group metals, potash, the rare earth elements group, tin, titanium, tungsten, uranium, vanadium, and zirconium, and allowed for faster permitting for domestic mining. This affected manufacturing in the fields of medicine, defense, the auto industry, electronics and communications, and space and aviation, among others.

By sourcing these minerals and elements in the U.S., President Trump ensured less dependence on countries like China, Japan, Mexico, Canada, Russia, South Korea, and Great Britain.

Reason 39. Real Prison Reform

In June 2018, President Trump commuted Alice Marie Johnson's 1996 life sentence for her first-time non-violent involvement in a Memphis cocaine trafficking organization. After serving twenty-one years, Johnson was released. This came after her failed plea to the Obama Administration for leniency and Johnson writing an op-ed for CNN asking for forgiveness and a second chance—words making an impact on President Trump. President Trump's son-in-law Jared Kushner and celebrity Kim Kardashian West brought the case to this President's attention. He would later pardon her in 2020.

In September 2018, President Trump met with celebrity Kim Kardashian West to discuss prison reform, following up on their successful effort to commute the sentence of Alice Marie Jackson. While Kardashian West advocated for the release of inmate Chris Young this time, President Trump's support for the wider-range reform program resulted in furthering progress with the First Step Act in November 2018.

President Trump continued to champion prison reform with Prison Fellowship and Senators Amy Klobuchar (D-MN) and Robert Portman (R-OH), Opportunity Zones, and his Pledge to American Workers.

Reason 40. Middle East Peace: Abraham Accords

President Trump's diplomatic gestures brought historic peace cooperation between Israel and the United Arab Emirates to normalize relations between the countries with the Abraham Accords in September 2020. This process was a long time in the works, with President Trump's son-in-law Jared Kushner playing a pivotal role, and President Trump brokering the deal. The signing ceremony was hosted at the White House on September 15, 2020, between President Trump, the United Arab Emirates, and Bahrain. This followed a September 13 meeting with President Trump, Prime Minister Benjamin Netanyahu of Israel, and Sheikh Mohammed Bin Zayed, Crown Prince of Abu Dhabi and Deputy Supreme Commander of the United Arab Emirates, and the peace deal between Israel and the Kingdom of Bahrain on September 11. This became the Abraham Accords: Declaration of Peace, Cooperation, and

Constructive Diplomatic and Friendly Relations between Israel and Arab Countries.

After the public announcement and show of cooperation, the Abraham Accords: Declaration of Peace, Cooperation, and Constructive Diplomatic and Friendly Relations between Israel and Arab Countries signees promoted "mutual understanding and coexistence, as well as respect for human dignity and freedom, including religious freedom. We encourage efforts to promote interfaith and intercultural dialogue to advance a culture of peace among the three Abrahamic religions and all humanity."

President Trump continues to seek peaceful alternatives at home and abroad.

Reason 41. Cuba

In December 2017, President Trump signed a Memorandum on Strengthening the Policy of the United States Toward Cuba. In it, he emphasized the need to provide relief to the people of Cuba while not supporting their communist governing. He outlined ending economic practices that benefited the Cuban government or military, intelligence, security agencies, and personnel over of the Cuban people.

This included a statutory ban on tourism, an economic embargo of Cuba (as outlined in Cuban Liberty and Democratic Solidarity (LIBERTAD) Act of 1996), support for the Cuban people through internet services expansion, a free press, free enterprise, free association, and lawful travel. The Memorandum also forbids the "Wet Foot, Dry Foot" policy that encouraged illegal immigration, and demanded the return of fugitives fleeing American justice who lived in Cuba.

Reason 42. Dealing with China

President Trump began America's new tenuous relationship with China in the spring of 2017, with a few phone calls with President Xi Jinping of the People's Republic of China. This was followed by meeting at the G20 Summit in Hamburg, Germany in July 2017. Dealing with North Korea and denuclearizing the Korean Peninsula were among the topics discussed.

Trade talks with China got friendlier by January 2018. President Trump spoke with President Xi Jinping by phone that month to discuss escalating events on the Korean Peninsula. Both expressed hope to change North Korea to a less dangerous nation. President Trump committed to U.S. maximum pressure for North Korea's denuclearization. The unbalanced trade issues—favoring China—were also discussed. President Trump planned to address China's theft of intellectual property and possible tariffs on aluminum imports in the future. Due to a leap in the trade deficit with China (Commerce Department report from November 2017 shows the deficit grew to $33.5 billion in China's favor), President Trump would decide over the next ninety days whether to tack on higher tariffs on imported steel.

In 2018, President Trump's diplomatic approach to China warmed. President Trump thanked Chinese President Xi at the Boao Forum for Asia conference for plans to allow foreign companies (U.S.) greater access to China's financial and manufacturing sectors and marketing platforms, perhaps hinting at lower automobile tariffs. This came in response to the growing possibilities of a destructive trade war brewing with the U.S. President Xi also pledged to lift limits on foreign investments in several sectors. President Trump thanked President Xi for his help in furthering progress for a future meeting with North Korean Supreme Leader Kim Jong-un.

When President Trump spoke by phone with President Xi Jinping on May 6, 2018, it was regarding developments on the Korean Peninsula. They also spoke on President Xi's meeting with Kim Jong-un and the need to continue sanctions until North Korea's nuclear and missile programs were dismantled. President Trump also reaffirmed his intent to balance trade between China and the U.S., and as time progressed, he stood his ground.

In December 2018, President Trump and President Xi Jinping met at the G-20 summit in Argentina, during which President Trump agreed to delay a 25 percent tariff scheduled to take effect January 2019, on $200 billion in Chinese goods. This came in hopes of better relations between the two countries, but did not rule out implementing the tariff in the future. Weeks later in the month, President Trump spoke by phone with President Xi and reported that the deal was moving along well. Among the deal details were stopping export of fentanyl to the U.S. and severe punishments for those traffickers who did.

When President Trump spoke by phone with President Xi Jinping about new activity related to North Korea, both welcomed a dialogue between the U.S. and North Korea. They agreed to keep sanctions against the country until complete and irreversible denuclearization was verified.

By March 2018, President Xi Jinping's term limits for president were removed, essentially making him president for life. (Russia's President Vladimir Putin began refining legislation in January 2020 that allowed him to stay in office through 2036.)

In May 2018, President Trump and President Xi Jinping had their respective constructive consultants hammer out the details to frame better trade deals benefiting both countries. Among the delegates were Secretary of the Treasury Steven T. Mnuchin, Secretary of Commerce Wilbur L. Ross, and United States Trade Representative Robert E. Lighthizer. Leading the

Chinese team was State Council Vice Premier Liu He, Special Envoy of President Xi. With the proper people at the table, the details started to take shape. Part of the bargaining was meeting the Chinese people's growing consumption needs. China agreed to increase purchases from the U.S., which offered an abundance of pork and other livestock and crops (including soybeans), as well as manufactured goods, automobiles, and equipment. In exchange, the demand for products would increase U.S. employment. Existing U.S. steel and aluminum tariffs on China, however, would still remain in effect.

Trade was slow to open wider on China's side. Seeing the sluggish response from President Xi on opening up markets in China to U.S. imports and continuing unfair practices during the summer of 2018, President Trump green-lighted $34 billion in tariffs on Chinese goods. This surprised China officials, and jump-started quicker responses.

Trade and prosperity between the two countries kept better pace for months, then a year, with a few bumps and bruises.

On January 15, 2020, as signing of the U.S.-China Phase One Trade Agreement commenced, President Trump, Vice Premier Liu, and Ambassador Cui Tiankai seemed to look to a prosperous future for both nations. A letter from President Xi Jinping, not present, was read to commemorate the agreement. However, as COVID-19 hit U.S. shores and spread from China (albeit the source and origin are still taking shape at the time of this writing), that trade deal soured.

By end of January 2020, am arrival suspension was placed on travelers from China. And as more was learned about COVID-19, President Trump let the trade significance with China relax as the communist country's ideology became starkly apparent.

Reason 43. North Korea

In August 2017, President Trump approved H.R. 3364 / Public Law No. 115–44 Countering America's Adversaries Through Sanctions Act, which included North Korea. On September 21, 2017, he also signed Executive Order 13810-Imposing Additional Sanctions With Respect to North Korea.

During this time, heading into the next year, President Trump, working with President Xi Jinping, pressured North Korean Supreme Leader Kim Jong-un into lessening and even halting the aggressive behavior toward Japan and the surrounding areas.

By June 2018, President Trump met with North Korean Supreme Leader Kim Jong-un in a historical outreach to the dictatorial socialist country. After being closed off from most of the world, the two leaders met at the 2018 North Korea-United States Singapore Summit on June 12. The results of the run-up to these talks were North Korea's suspension of missile and nuclear testing. North Korean plane fly-bys of Japan had already ceased. The talks produced some promises on North Korea's part to close and dismantle Punggye-ri Nuclear Test Site with the potential of full denuclearization. President Trump, in return, stated his hope for cessation of joint military exercises with South Korea and the pullout of U.S. forces from South Korea. A second summit was planned for 2019, and those details would begin in September 2018.

During President Trump and Kim Jong-un's June 2018 summit, North Korea reaffirmed its commitment for complete denuclearization, agreed to help the United States recover POW remains, and committed to destroying a missile engine-testing site. While North Korea did return American POW remains and video was released of missile engine-testing site being destroyed, denuclearization was not wholly confirmed.

In July 2018, President Trump approved H.R. 2061 / Public Law No. 115–198 North Korean Human Rights Reauthorization Act of 2017. This Law allowed better information and research into North Korea's human rights and treatment (sponsored by Representative Ileana Ros-Lehtinen, R-FL).

In June 2019, President Trump met with Leader Kim Jong-un near the South Korea border with North Korea in the village of Panmunjom in the Demilitarized Zone for a third summit. In the meeting, President Trump impressed upon the leader the prosperity that could be North Korea's once working-level talks were achieved. To show good faith, President Trump walked alongside Kim Jong-un into North Korea through the military demarcation line marking the edges of the two Koreas, the first sitting president to do so.

President Trump signed more sanctions in the form of North Korea Sanctions Regulations in April 2020, as denuclearization of North Korea continues to be decided. Speaking relations continue, too—far from the "war with North Korea" some politicians touted when Candidate Trump ran in 2016.

Reason 44. A Better KORUS Deal

In March 2017, President Trump signed Executive Order EO 13785- Establishing Enhanced Collection and Enforcement of Antidumping and Countervailing Duties and Violations of Trade and Customs Laws, curtailing cheap goods from flooding the U.S. and stiffening the enforcement of Intellectual Property Rights protection laws.

In November 2017, the Korea Chamber of Commerce and Industry reported that 24 South Korean companies would purchase U.S. products and services worth $57.5 billion, including $22.8 billion in energy sectors, by 2021. Korea also agreed to buy more U.S. military equipment, including the F-35A joint strike fighters, and to upgrade KF-16 fighter jets, as well as Patriot PAC-3 ballistic missiles to address the U.S. trade deficit with South Korea. The previous deal had allowed a jump of over $6.3 billion in 2012 to $9.8 billion in 2017, more than 50 percent, in South Korea's favor.

President Trump followed up on the KORUS-FTA in September 2018. In it, South Korea allowed double the annual number of American automobiles—from 25,000 to 50,000 per manufacturer year. South Korea's steel imports to the United States will also be limited.

Reason 45. The Iran Deal

Quitting the Iran nuclear deal, the Joint Comprehensive Plan of Action (JCPOA). In May 2018, President Trump signed the National Security Presidential Memorandum on Ceasing United States Participation in the Joint Comprehensive Plan of Action and Taking Additional Action To Counter Iran's Malign Influence and Deny Iran All Paths to a Nuclear Weapon, and in that August, also signed Executive Order EO 13846-Reimposing Certain Sanctions With Respect to Iran. This Executive Order used the President's International Emergency Economic Powers Act and Constitutional and other powers to re-impose sanctions against Iran that were lifted by the Obama Administration's 2015 JCPOA. This bill effectively blocked the government of Iran from purchasing or acquiring U.S. bank notes or precious metals and denied "certain Iranian persons".

Reason 46. Trans-Pacific Partnership

In January 2017, President Trump signed the Presidential Memorandum Regarding Withdrawal of the United States from the Trans-Pacific Partnership Negotiations and Agreement

(TPP). This took the U.S. out of the deal that put American interests on a lopsided trade agreement benefitting other countries. President Trump left the door to TPP open, remaining flexible to better options. On February 23, 2018, President Trump commented during a joint news conference that the United States might rejoin the Trans-Pacific Partnership if it offered a better deal for the U.S.

Reason 47. Paris Climate Accord

On June 1, 2017, President Trump announced the U.S. Withdrawal From the Paris Climate Accord. The Energy Information Administration's 2017 Annual Energy Outlook reported that, from 2005 to 2016, energy related carbon dioxide emissions fell at an average annual rate of 1.4%. These emissions were projected to continue to fall from 2016 to 2040. At the same time, the EIA reported that emissions in the developing countries of the world, like China and India, were expected to double their 2005 levels by 2040—canceling out any "progress" the U.S. was making in regard to emissions. According to National Economic Research Associates (NERA) analysis, continued commitment under the Paris Climate Accord would cost the U.S. nearly $3 trillion by 2040. By that date, the U.S. economy could lose 6.5 million industrial sector jobs, including 3.1 million manufacturing jobs, hitting industries like cement, iron and steel, coal, natural gas, and petroleum the worst.

This was a promise kept.

Reason 48. Empowering Women

In support of women in pioneering and innovated fields, President Trump approved H.R. 255 / Public Law No. 115–6

Promoting Women in Entrepreneurship Act in February 2017 (sponsored by Representative Elizabeth H. Esty, D-CT).

He also approved H.R. 321 / Public Law No. 115–7 Inspiring the Next Space Pioneers, Innovators, Researchers, and Explorers (INSPIRE) Women Act (sponsored by Representative Barbara Comstock (R-VA), which included the NASA GIRLS and NASA BOYS programs in January 2017, and approved S. 3247 / Public Law No. 115–428 Women's Entrepreneurship and Economic Empowerment Act of 2018, which modified U.S. Agency for International Development (USAID) programs to provide targeted assistance for women in January 2019 (sponsored by Senator John Boozman, R-AR).

Reason 49. STEM

In September 2017, under President Trump's push for STEM programs in America, private sector companies pledged $300 million to K-12 computer science programs. Companies included Amazon at $50 million, Facebook at $50 million, Google at $50 million, Microsoft at $50 million, and Salesforce at $50 million. Lockheed Martin pledged $25 million. Accenture, General Motors, and Pluralsight each offered $10 million or more.

STEM also advanced women in space programs. In 2018, President Trump approved H.R. 4254 / Public Law No. 115–303 Women in Aerospace Education Act, which amended the National Science Foundation Authorization Act of 2002 to allow grants awarded by the National Science Foundation (NSF) to provide internships for eligible undergraduate freshman and sophomore students in research at national laboratories and NASA centers. This approval included NASA to encourage recruitment of qualified female candidates underrepresented in the science, technology, engineering, mathematics, and computer science fields. (Sponsored by Representative Stephen Knight, R-CA.)

Reason 50. Remembering Suffrage

On February 15, 2018, President Trump signed a Statement on Susan B. Anthony Day, 2018. This would be followed roughly eighteen months later with President Trump posthumously pardoning the women's suffrage visionary on the 100th anniversary of the movement.

Reason 51. Education and School Choice

President Trump held several listening sessions to get input from education experts and home educators. In February 2018, he listened to parents and teachers from diverse facets of schooling, including homeschooling parent Laura Parrish from Virginia, charter school parent Mary Riner of DC, Jennifer Coleman from Virginia (mother and homeschooler of six), Julie Baumann (special education teacher) from New Jersey, Bartholomew Cirenzav (with seven children in both private and public schools), Jane Quennville (principal of a special education center in Virginia), and Ken Smith (educator for at-risk kids), and Education Secretary Betsy DeVos.

In April 2017, President Trump signed Executive Order EO 13791-Enforcing Statutory Prohibitions on Federal Control of Education, ensuring states to keep control of education in their state rather than cede to the Federal government.

In March 2019, President Trump signed Executive Order EO 13864-Improving Free Inquiry, Transparency, and Accountability at Colleges and Universities. This provides more affordability, transparency, and accountability in the governance in education. It pressed for institutions of higher education to be accountable for student outcomes and student life on campus. President Trump also insisted on promoting free and open debate on college and university campuses, deeming free inquiry an essential feature to democracy in the U.S. It also promoted learning, scientific discovery, and economic prosperity.

During the COVID-19 crisis of 2020, President Trump signed Proclamation 9994 of March 13, 2020 (Declaring a National Emergency Concerning the Novel Coronavirus Disease (COVID-19) Outbreak), and within that scope, provided immediate student loan borrower relief during the pandemic by both suspending loan payments and temporarily setting interest rates to 0 percent. This was scheduled to expire on September 30, 2020, but President Trump extended it on student loans held by the Department of Education until December 31, 2020.

President Trump continues to push Congress to pass the Education Freedom Scholarships and Opportunity Act in 2020, and give one million children the freedom to attend a school of their choice. This school choice plan has more than 120 Congressional co-sponsors. This would create a $5 billion annual tax credit for donations to state-based, locally-controlled scholarships to help families pay for tuition, dual enrollment, out-of-district transportation, tutoring, and apprenticeships.

Reason 52. Smarter FDA Practices

In late 2017, President Trump approved H.R. 4374 / Public Law No. 115–92 To amend the Federal Food, Drug, and Cosmetic Act to authorize additional emergency uses for medical products to reduce deaths and the severity of injuries caused by agents of war (and for other purposes). This freed up medical products for uses other than their intended purpose, expanding the U.S. health fields. This was pivotal in the later COVID-19 crisis.

Reason 53. Auto Industry Revival

With President Trump's promise to open up unnecessary regulations, America's auto industry got its wheels back. In January 2017, the General Motors Co. confirmed investing $1 billion into its U.S. manufacturing and pledged more U.S. jobs, plus bringing more small parts production jobs from Mexico back to the U.S. Hyundai Motor Co. pledged another $3.1 billion in existing American manufacturing.

Also in January 2017, Toyota Motor announced its $10 billion investment plan in the U.S. over the next five years. Later in January, Toyota Motor Corp would add 400 jobs and invest $600 million for retooling in an Indiana assembly plant. In August 2017, Toyota and Mazda announced a joint venture plan to build a $1.6 billion U.S. assembly plant, later announcing the location as Huntsville, Alabama. The plant was expected to manufacture 300,000 vehicles a year and employ 4,000 workers. The plant has a planned open date of 2021. A 1,100-acre plant had been planned, but was upgraded to over 2,500-acres, doubling its footprint.

Along with traditional fossil fuel powered vehicles, more models were built as hybrids and electric, adding to the diversity of fuel options.

President Trump kept his promise to bring automotive manufacturing jobs back to the U.S.

Reason 54. Better Trade Fairness

After listening to representatives in the steel and aluminum industries, President Trump forged new trade agreements in America's favor. After years of cheap metals from importers bring "dumped" on American shores, making U.S. made metals unable to compete, President Trump signed a Memorandum on

Steel Imports and Threats to National Security on April 20, 2017. This placed over 150 antidumping and countervailing duty orders on steel products. This was an action he would revisit often over the next few years, keeping abreast and ahead of the threat of steel and aluminum imports.

On March 8, 2018, President Trump took another look at the adjustment in the Presidential Memorandum regarding the Trade Expansion Act of 1962 (and other years) after a report declared the present quantities of aluminum imports and the circumstances of global excess capacity for producing aluminum were "weakening our internal economy," leaving the United States "almost totally reliant on foreign producers of primary aluminum" and "at risk of becoming completely reliant on foreign producers of high-purity aluminum that is essential for key military and commercial systems", according to White House documents. President Trump stiffened the tariffs accordingly.

In May 2019, President Trump signed Executive Order EO 13871-Imposing Sanctions With Respect to the Iron, Steel, Aluminum, and Copper Sectors of Iran. This affected Executive Order 12957, March 15, 1995. In a series of tariffs and limits, President Trump reined in the dumping and glutting of offshore metal flooding the U.S. markets.

In signing Executive Order EO 13796-Addressing Trade Agreement Violations and Abuses and Executive Order EO 13797 of April 29, 2017, Establishment of Office of Trade and Manufacturing Policy (OTMP) within the White House Office, President Trump placed emphasis on American steel and aluminum (Buy American and Hire American, described in Executive Order 13788 of April 18, 2017).

American metalworkers were ready for the changes a Trump presidency would bring. In March 2018, U.S. Steel announced it would reopen steelmaking facilities and one of two blast furnaces at its Granite City, Illinois plant. This required 500 new employees. Officials for the company cited President Trump's tariffs on steel and aluminum imports. Jobs blasted back in March 2018 for Century Aluminum Co. in Kentucky, announcing it would restart smelter lines in the state and double its workforce to 600 workers.

President Trump continued to protect U.S. metalworkers by signing Proclamation 9704-Adjusting Imports of Aluminum into the United States, and Proclamation 9705-Adjusting Imports of Steel into the United States in March 2018.

Reason 55. U.S. Worker Force

President Trump continued to support other natural and renewable sources of energy, even as unemployment hit a 50-year low (pre-COVID-19). While the projected fastest growing jobs were *predicted* to be in wind turbine service technicians and solar photovoltaic installers for 2016-2026, the most new jobs added *expectations* from 2016-2026 will be in construction, carpentry, and other construction and engineering trades. The month of August 2018 saw a record number of jobs posted by employers since December 2000, reaching 7.14 million, amid a fifty-year low in unemployment.

In July 2018, President Trump signed Executive Order EO 13845-Establishing the President's National Council for the American Worker, "to provide a coordinated process for developing a national strategy to ensure that America's students and workers have access to affordable, relevant, and innovative education and job training that will equip them to compete and win in the global economy, and for monitoring the implementation of that strategy".

The Order stated: "We need to prepare Americans for the 21st century economy and the emerging industries of the future. We must foster an environment of lifelong learning and skills-based training, and cultivate a demand-driven approach to workforce development. My Administration will champion effective, results-driven education and training so that American students and workers can obtain the skills they need to succeed in the jobs of today and of the future."

With the Policy being: "[for] the executive branch to work with private employers, educational institutions, labor unions, other non-profit organizations, and State, territorial, tribal, and local governments to update and reshape our education and job training landscape so that it better meets the needs of American students, workers, and businesses."

President Trump reaffirmed his dedication to the American worker in June 2020, by signing Executive Order EO 13931-Continuing the President's National Council for the American Worker and the American Workforce Policy Advisory Board.

As America comes out of the COVID-19 crisis, the economy rebounds, and these job needs are coming back.

Reason 56. Supporting Farmers and Agriculture

In July 2017, President Trump, Secretary of the Treasury Steve Mnunchin, and Director for the Office of Public Liaison George Sifakis met with agricultural industry leaders to discuss economic growth, what they needed in the new GOP tax plan, regulatory relief, higher trade incentives, and a simplified tax code. By FY2018, under President Trump, the USDA eliminated eight onerous regulations, saving farmers almost $400 million.

President Trump helped farming families keep their land in their families after death without devastating estate taxes and penalties by passing relief measures. In December 2017, President Trump signed H.R. 1 The Tax Cuts and Jobs Act (the GOP tax bill) to temporarily double estate tax exemptions through the year 2025. Other legislature is currently in progress, including S.215 Death Tax Repeal Act of 2019 (sponsored by Senator John Thune, R-SD) and H.R. 5422 Death Tax Repeal Act (sponsored by Representative Jason Smith, R-MO), to make the exemption permanent. In April 2017, President Trump signed Executive Order EO 13790-Promoting Agriculture and Rural Prosperity in America.

When trade talks with China threatened to get tough in the summer of 2018, President Trump looked out for American farmers by sending aid from China's tariffs with a $12 billion package of agricultural assistance. President Trump also announced several programs for the government to buy surplus farm produce for federal assistance programs. These came in the form of the Food Purchase and Distribution Program to purchase surplus fruits, nuts, rice, legumes, beef, pork, and milk for distribution to food banks and other nutrition programs.

President Trump supported the future of farming by approving H.R. 439 / Public Law No. 116–7 National FFA Organization's Federal Charter Amendments Act in February 2019, promoting Future Farmers of America, the youth in farming.

In response to the 2017 listening session, in June 2019, President Trump signed Executive Order EO 13874-Modernizing the Regulatory Framework for Agricultural Biotechnology Products, to help farmers raise better crops to feed the U.S. and the world, in many cases, without undue regulatory burdens, while protecting their croplands and harnessing new technologies.

President Trump continues to work on behalf of America's hardworking farming families, winning arguments against the WTO on their behalf, and awaiting beneficial legislation to sign from Congress.

Reason 57. Supporting U.S. Ranchers

In the summer of 2017, President Trump was able to end China's ban on U.S. cattle and opened a market of 1.4 billion people to American-produced beef. For the first time in nearly 14 years, U.S. cattle producers had access to a huge market that purchased roughly $2.5 billion in beef a year. By 2018, U.S. beef exports to China and South Korea rose by $1 billion to over $8.33 billion—a new record high—with a 15 percent increase in dollars.

President Trump's rebalancing trade in North America through the USMCA on September 30, 2018, made better deals for American farmers and ranchers and supporting industries, increasing broilers (chickens), chickens, turkey, and the hatching egg trade. Processed products like yogurt, buttermilk, cheese, and other forms, and less processed products like fluid milk, whey, and butter products had structured tariffs and ensured long-term trade with Canada and Mexico.

In August 2019, President Trump signed the U.S.-EU Trade Agreement to reduce and limit trade tariffs. This allowed more U.S. beef into European Union and permitted duty-free American beef exports to the EU within a year, allowing an increase of 46 percent and another 90 percent within seven years. This would make duty-free exports rise from $150 million to $420 million (over 180 percent increase). Beef and agricultural markets also opened wider, including more U.S. beef to Japanese markets and expanding markets in Tunisia, Morocco, and Australia.

Despite strained relations between the U.S. and China, President Trump stayed strong on tariffs, and China made good on trade deals in the livestock and crop markets. As of April 23, 2020, the USDA reported China purchasing 1,400 metric tons of U.S. beef in addition to the 1,500-ton purchase earlier in the month, which was a new record high purchase. This came after China agreed to push off trade restrictions. China also purchased 272,000 tons of U.S. soybeans as it allowed exemptions for their importers, and purchasing was expected to be up 43 percent over the previous year. By June 2020, China would import 70 percent more U.S. beef than it did pre-January 2019. In the first half of 2020, U.S pork exports were over 27 percent higher than a year ago due to larger purchases by China.

President Trump's dealing-making skills are paying off worldwide.

Reason 58. U.S. Fishing

Putting U.S. fishing in focus, President Trump approved H.R. 4528 / Public Law No. 115–228 To make technical amendments to certain marine fish conservation statutes, and for other purposes, in August 2018. Before the bill was signed, billfish caught by U.S. vessels and unloaded on shore in Hawaii or Pacific Insular Areas (American Samoa, Baker Island, Guam, Howland Island, Jarvis Island, Johnston Atoll, Kingman Reef, Midway Island, the Northern Mariana Islands, Palmyra Atoll, and Wake Island) were allowed to be sold and exported to non-U.S. markets or sent to other U.S. markets. With President Trump's signing of this bill, billfish caught by U.S. vessels and unloaded (landed) in Hawaii or Pacific Insular Areas are required to be sold in those markets (Hawaii or Pacific Insular Areas). Billfish include sailfish, marlin, and swordfish. (Sponsored by Representative Darren Soto, D-FL.)

In May 2020, President Trump signed Executive Order 13921-Promoting American Seafood Competitiveness and Economic Growth. This protected U.S. food supplies by identifying and removing unnecessary regulatory barriers restricting American fishermen and the fish industry while also combating illegal, unreported, and unregulated fishing, and promoted fair and reciprocal trade in seafood products.

President Trump also got better deals for U.S. commercial fishermen in lobster, crab, and other fishing and seafood industries. At a roundtable for commercial fishermen in June 2020 held in Maine, President Trump heard from fishermen on their needs to lift restrictions to sell to China, Canada, Europe, and the Far East to level trade imbalances. To compound offshore problems, late Obama-era decisions had closed off 5,000 square miles of ocean off the coast of Maine, cutting out U.S. commercial fishermen. In June 2020, President Trump signed Proclamation 10049 modifying the decision, removing the crippling restrictions on U.S. commercial fishing in Proclamation 9496 (Northeast Canyons and Seamounts Marine National Monument in the Atlantic Ocean) signed in 2016. This allowed well-regulated U.S. commercial fishing in the 4,913 square miles of the United States Exclusive Economic Zone.

President Trump also signed a Memorandum on Protecting the United States Lobster Industry in June 2020, protecting the U.S. lobster industry against China's "unjust retaliatory tariffs designed strategically to inflict financial harm on America's farmers, fishermen, and workers in other industries." In these new tariffs, China had agreed that seafood, including lobsters, would be one of the products China agreed to purchase, making exclusions from its retaliatory tariffs for imports of U.S. lobster.

President Trump continues to work for fair seafood trade, and follows up with appropriate measures to enforce agreements made with foreign markets.

Reason 59. Rural Broadband

On January 8, 2018, President Trump signed Executive Order EO 13821-Presidential Executive Order on Streamlining and Expediting Requests to Locate Broadband Facilities in Rural America, and in February of 2018, approved S. 96 / Public Law

No. 115–129 Improving Rural Call Quality and Reliability Act of 2017. These measures helped bring more stability to rural cyberspace and helped connect the vastness of America. This worked with President Trump's Memorandum Supporting Broadband Tower Facilities in Rural America on Federal Properties Managed by the Department of the Interior.

These changes would benefit rural areas later as President Trump signed Executive Order EO 13941-Improving Rural Health and Telehealth Access in August 2020, keeping on the COVID-19 upgrade of "home-based" doctor checks (which also works with Social Security). This was addressed in President Trump's America-First Healthcare Plan announced in September 2020.

Reason 60. The Economy

In March 2017, President Trump held a listening session with Treasury Secretary Steven Mnuchin and National Economic Council Director Gary Cohn and banking interests to discuss how better to help U.S. businesses keep and expand business in America. In mid-April 2017, President Trump signed Executive Order EO 13788-Buy American and Hire American, to promote American-made products and goods, fueling the economy with U.S. jobs.

After that discussion, President Trump had his administration look into removing business-strangling regulations. This enabled reshoring of big business money home to the U.S., bring jobs back to America, lower taxes, and open up more non-college careers for younger workers. The stock market ran as a healthy foundation for these changes. The end result was that the economy righted itself to give all workers a better chance at good jobs and a brighter future.

In 2018, poverty rates for African Americans and Hispanic Americans hit new lows. Wages rose faster for the bottom ten percent of earners than for the top 10 percent of earners, and the bottom half of households grew by 47 percent, over three times the rate of increase for the top one percent of households.

By February 2020, real GDP growth under President Trump beat the Congressional Budget Office's (CBO) projections each year, exceeded the Obama Administration's expansion rate, and added five million more jobs than the CBO had projected prior to the 2016 election. Seven million jobs have been created nationwide under President Trump's presidency, including over 500,000 manufacturing jobs. Record low numbers in unemployment came for African Americans, Hispanic Americans, Asian Americans, Americans without a high school degree, and disabled Americans during this time.

To get this thriving economy going again past the COVID-19 devastation, President Trump announced the Great American Economic Revival Industry Groups. These included authorities like Zippy Duvall of the American Farm Bureau Federation, Jim Collins of Corteva Agriscience, Jamie Dimon of JPMorgan Chase, Sean McGarvey of North America's Building Trades Union, Linda Bauer Darr of American Council of Engineering Companies, Marillyn Hewson from Lockheed Martin, Phebe Novakovic of General Dynamics, Tom Fanning of Southern Company, Ross Perot Jr of Perot Group and Hillwood, Abigail Johnson of Fidelity Investments, Marvin Irby of National Restaurant Association, Wolfgang Puck, Carlos Abrams-Rivera from Kraft, Mike Roman from 3M, Robert Ford of Abbott Laboratories, David Wichmann from UnitedHealth Group, Geoff Ballotti of Wyndham Hotels & Resorts, Jim Umpleby III from Caterpillar, Bill Ford from Ford Motor Company, Mary Barra of General Motors Company, Elon Musk of Tesla, Jay Timmons from National Association of Manufacturers, Jeff Bezos of Amazon, Tim Cook of Apple, Mark Zuckerberg of Facebook, and leaders from Wal-Mart, Home Depot, CVS, IBM, Microsoft, Intel, Google/Alphabet Inc., Verizon, Comcast, FedEx, UPS, DHL, numerous sports leaders, and a long list of thought leaders, among many others.

Reason 61. Elder Care

In mid-October 2017, President Trump approved S. 178 / Public Law No. 115–70 Elder Abuse Prevention and Prosecution Act, to help protect America's seniors and keep their dignity. To keep this in force, every one of the 93 U.S. Attorney's Offices will have a coordinator to focus solely on fraud against elders.

In March 2020, after a roundtable discussion at the White House, President Trump added the National Elder Fraud Hotline to the DOJ to help fight the $2.2 billion fraud against senior problems. President Trump also demanded more stringent COVID-19 safety measures, requiring nursing homes to test their staff twice a week, weekly, or monthly (according to individual facility risk of transmission), and test residents and staff when new cases arise. The Trump Administration provided point-of-care (POC) testing devices and supplies of test kits to get the nursing homes quickly engaged. By August 2020, over two million POC tests and 5,600 POC machines had been sent to the nursing homes with the highest risks. In the face of the COVID-19 impact, Medicare telehealth services were expanded for seniors. President Trump demanded more accountability from state governors on how they handled Coronavirus cases among nursing homes in their states. President Trump also made sure nursing homes had the Personal Protection Equipment (PPE) supplies, training, and financial aid needed for these homes.

In July 2020, President Trump continued looking out for seniors by signing Executive Order EO 13938-Increasing Drug Importation To Lower Prices for American Patients. This allowed importing of safe, lower cost prescription drugs and insulin for American patients.

Reason 62. African American History

In February 2017, President Trump held a listening session with leaders in the African American communities to better understand their needs, concerns, and interests. Coming away from this, he lent his signature to several pieces of legislature that commemorated outstanding, pivotal, and history-changing men and women in Black history.

In early November 2017, President Trump approved H.R. 2989 / Public Law No. 115–77 Frederick Douglass Bicentennial Commission Act. This bill established the Frederick Douglass Bicentennial Commission, allowing it to plan, develop, and carry out programs and activities to honor Frederick Douglass (born 1817 into slavery) for the bicentennial anniversary of his birth, and recommend the federal government entities appropriate to carry out such programs and activities.

The bill was sponsored by Congresswoman Eleanor Holmes Norton (D-DC), and was brought twice before to Congress. The bill was introduced February 11, 2014, but did not receive a vote during that session. It was again brought forward February 11, 2016, but also died without a vote. Joining Congresswoman Eleanor Holmes Norton for the 2017 attempt was Congressman Andy Harris (R-MD), and Senators Chris Van Hollen (D-MD) and Ben Cardin (D-MD). The 16-member commission was made up of two members appointed by the President, four members appointed by the President on the recommendation of each of the Mayor of the District of Columbia and the Governors of Maryland, Massachusetts, and New York, three members (at least one of whom must be a Member of the House) appointed by the Speaker of the House, three members (at least one of whom must be a Senator) appointed by the Senate Majority Leader, two members (at least one of whom must be a Member of the House) appointed by the House Minority Leader, and two members (at least one of whom must be a Senator) appointed by the Senate Minority

Leader. President Trump also made a Statement on Signing the Frederick Douglass Bicentennial Commission Act.

In January 2018, President Trump signed H.R. 1242 / Public Law No. 115–102 400 Years of African-American History Commission Act, to observe the 400th anniversary of the 1619 arrival of Africans in the English colonies at Point Comfort, Virginia, and show the ensuing struggle, freedom, and future contributions made (sponsored by Representative Robert C. Scott, D-VA).

President Trump also signed H.R. 1927 / Public Law No. 115–104 African American Civil Rights Network Act of 2017 in January 2018, requiring the Department of the Interior to create a U.S. Civil Rights Network within the National Park Service (NPS) to include all NPS programs relating to the African American civil rights movement from 1939 through 1968 (sponsored by Representative Wm. Lacy Clay, D-MO).

President Trump supported a high school project that led to a law. In January 2019, President Trump approved S. 3191 / Public Law No. 115–426 Civil Rights Cold Case Records Collection Act of 2018. This unique law originated through the efforts of Hightstown High School students in New Jersey in 2015. The students pushed to examine closed civil rights murder cases. The bill forms a Civil Rights Cold Case Records Review Board as an independent agency made up of impartial private citizens. The bill also requires the National Archives and Records Administration (NARA) to provide more transparency to these sensitive cases. The law provides for review and possible release of records of criminal investigations related to alleged Federal civil rights violations between 1940 and 1980 ("cold case records"). This bill was sponsored by Senator Doug Jones (D-AL) and found additional support from Senators Ted Cruz (R-TX) and Kamala Harris (D-CA), and former Senator Claire McCaskill (D-MO).

Reason 63. Addressing DACA

On December 5, 2017, the Trump Administration began plans to wind down the Deferred Action for Childhood Arrivals program and as a result, those currently covered would begin losing their protection and work permits on March 6, 2018. This is a battle President Trump is currently fighting, sometimes with the U.S. Supreme Court, as he strives to find a fair and legal path for the DACA program within U.S. immigration laws.

Reason 64. State Support

In April 2017, President Trump signed Executive Order EO 13791-Enforcing Statutory Prohibitions on Federal Control of Education, ensuring states keep control of education in their state rather than surrender it to the Federal government.

In mid-May 2017, President Trump approved S. 496 / Public Law No. 115–33 To repeal the rule issued by the Federal Highway Administration and the Federal Transit Administration entitled "Metropolitan Planning Organization Coordination and Planning Area Reform." This Act would have made MPOs consolidate or absorb surrounding areas. Repealing this Act from December 20, 2016, leaves more control to the states and allows more free choice of residence to individuals.

President Trump also stepped in with federal aid when disasters struck states, including Hurricanes Harvey, Irma, and Maria (2017) and Hurricane Laura (2020) and sent Federal aid to Louisiana and other states and regions up and down the East Coast. President Trump made available disaster/emergency funds to Oregon and other states and tribal areas and localities for recovery efforts due to the wildfires and straight-line winds (September 7, 2020). In America's heartland, severe storms in

August 2020 left heavy damage. President Trump declared a major disaster in Iowa and responded with Federal aid to rebuild, replace, and provide relief. In 2020, President Trump sent aid to numerous states for wildfires, hurricanes, severe storms, earthquakes, flooding, straight-line winds, and other major natural disasters.

California has been especially plagued by wildfires, caused naturally, by arson, and also through neglect over the last few decades. As recent as 2018, San Francisco was concerned about the unchecked abundant overgrowth of vegetation and kindling-dry undergrowth in California. The dry stretches and droughts, coupled with the cutback in controlled burning, increasing fuel loads, and change in approach to vegetation management (or lack thereof), turned many areas into fire-ready spaces. By not clearing dead and dry vegetation for the "normal nature" approach, California has had increasingly devastating fires sweeping large expanses of land—that oddly stop at Canada's border. California wildfires skyrocketed in 2020 to over three million acres from January 2020 to September 18, 2020.

Since the beginning of the year (2020), wildfires have burned over 3.1 million acres in California. This year's acres burned are 26 times higher than the acres burned in 2019 for the same time period. California's top five worst wildfires have happened since 2018.

In December 2018, President Trump signed Executive Order EO 13855-Promoting Active Management of America's Forests, Rangelands, and Other Federal Lands To Improve Conditions and Reduce Wildfire Risk. This included "Reducing vegetation giving rise to wildfire conditions through forest health treatments by increasing health treatments as part of DOI's offering for sale 600 million board feet of timber" and "Treating 3.5 million acres of Department of Agriculture (USDA) Forest Service (FS) lands to reduce fuel load".

Despite not following the Order, President Trump approved emergency aid to California for wildfire disaster relief on December 2017, August 2018, November 2018, August 2020, and numerous times within those dates.

Reason 65. Fighting Human Trafficking

Following a listening session in February 2017, President Trump approved S. 1862 / Public Law No. 115–427 Trafficking Victims Protection Reauthorization Act of 2017. This Reauthorization Act (TVPRA) allowed for the safe and humane return of illegally-smuggled minors back to their families in their home countries. He also approved H.R. 2200 / Public Law No. 115–425 Frederick Douglass Trafficking Victims Prevention and Protection Reauthorization Act of 2018 in January 2019.

As the U.S.-Mexico border tightened to illegal crossings, President Trump signed Executive Order EO 13867-Issuance of Permits With Respect to Facilities and Land Transportation Crossings at the International Boundaries of the United States in April 2019. This allowed trade and legal access to the border while blocking human trafficking.

In January 2020, President Trump signed Executive Order EO 13903-Combating Human Trafficking and Online Child Exploitation in the United States, to protect online users from predatory human traffickers using media.

Reason 66. Protecting the Environment

As America built up its workforce and manufacturing came home, President Trump safeguarded the environment and natural spaces, even with quicker permitting for projects (EO 13766-Expediting Environmental Reviews and Approvals for

High Priority Infrastructure Projects, signed soon after taking office in January 2017). In August 2017, President Trump signed Executive Order EO 13807-Establishing Discipline and Accountability in the Environmental Review and Permitting Process for Infrastructure Projects, to maintain healthy environments while considering the impact of new commercial and business growth.

He protected the U.S.'s waterfronts by signing Executive Order EO 13840-Ocean Policy To Advance the Economic, Security, and Environmental Interests of the United States, which also included the Great Lakes. Along with President Trump signing the S.47 John D. Dingell, Jr. Conservation, Management, and Recreation Act in March 2019, he also signed the Land and Water Conservation Fund Permanent Funding Act, providing $900 million yearly in permanent funding to the Land and Water Conservation Fund (LWCF).

Reason 67. U.S. Parks

President Trump proves his generosity and true love for America's lands. In March 2017, President Trump, who promised never to accept his president salary as personal payment (except that $1.00), donated his first-quarter salary to the National Park Service, which was slotted go toward restoring two projects at a national battlefield. (According to Cornell Law School, U.S. presidents must accept salaries, so President Trump agreed to be paid $1.00, leaving the balance to his choice of recipient.)

On December 21, 2018, President Trump signed Executive Order EO 13855-Promoting Active Management of America's Forests, Rangelands, and other Federal Lands to Improve Conditions and Reduce Wildfire Risk. These measures, including removal of underbrush and vegetation, reduce the risk of wildfires on Department of Interior-controlled lands, such as the ones California saw in recent decades (from 2000-

2019, California saw over 8,000 wildfires burn more than 720,000 acres). It also covered flooding damage, erosion control, and invasive species management.

On August 4, 2020, President Trump signed S. 3422 Great American Outdoors Act, which established National Parks and Public Land Legacy Restoration Fund. This also restored deferred maintenance funding for federal lands (from previous administrations), and for FY2021-FY2025, required deposits into the National Parks and Public Land Legacy Restoration Fund in an amount equal to 50 percent of federal revenue made from oil, gas, coal and alternative/renewable energies from federal lands and water, up to 1.9 billion per fiscal year (sponsored by Senator Cory Gardner, R-CO).

The fund will be used for the National Park Service, the Forest Service, U.S. Fish and Wildlife Service, the Bureau of Land Management, and the Bureau of Indian Education.

President Trump also commemorated America's fight against slavery in his Proclamation 9811-Establishment of the Camp Nelson National Monument. This proclamation allows the National Park Service to commemorate the Civil War Camp Nelson in Kentucky as a living landmark for escaped and freed slaves and those soldiers who helped gain that freedom.

Reason 68. Foreign Terrorism

At the end of January 2018, President Trump signed Executive Order EO 13823-Protecting America Through Lawful Detention of Terrorists. This revoked EO 13492 of January 22, 2009, signed by President Obama, which emptied out the detainees and closed Guantánamo Bay Naval Base.

In March 2017, President Trump signed Executive Order EO 13780-Protecting the Nation From Foreign Terrorist Entry Into the United States, which "raised the baseline for the vetting and screening of foreign nationals, improved our ability to prevent the entry of malicious actors, and enhanced the security".

President Trump continued keeping America safe by approving S. 1595 / Public Law No. 115–272 Hizballah International Financing Prevention Amendments Act of 2018, imposing sanctions on foreign individuals or entities that knowingly support, engage with, or fund raise or recruit for certain Hezbollah-affiliated groups (sponsored by Senator Marco Rubio, R-FL).

In early January 2020, President Trump announced that Major General Qasem Soleimani, leader of the Quds Force, extraterritorial wing of the Islamic Revolutionary Guard Corps, had been killed in a precision drone strike. Soleimani was responsible for wounding and killing thousands of American and coalition service members. This followed an attack on the U.S. Embassy in Baghdad. In October 2019, ISIS leader Abu Bakr al-Baghdadi was killed in a special forces raid.

Within months, President Trump had presided over the elimination of two of the world's most dangerous terrorists.

Reason 69. Protecting America

In May 2019, President Trump signed Executive Order EO 13873-Securing the Information and Communications Technology and Services Supply Chain. This encompassed exploitable vulnerabilities in information, communications, technology, and other services. Leisure apps such as TikTok and WeChat, both influenced by the Communist Chinese government, would be addressed in later legislation.

In March 2019, President Trump also signed Executive Order EO 13865-Coordinating National Resilience to Electromagnetic Pulses, which safeguards the U.S. from electromagnetic pulses (EMP) in natural and manmade forms.

These have long been a concern, with the possibility to affect everything from automobiles, cell phones, and smart appliances to air control, city infrastructure, and communications.

Reason 70. Drug-Free Youth

President Trump continued the Drug-Free Communities (DFC) Support Program (since 1997), which operates under the White House Office of National Drug Control Policy (ONDCP)*, and released an encouraging 2020 Drug-Free Communities report, including:

27 percent decline in prescription drug misuse among high school students.
45 percent decline in tobacco use among high school students.
46 percent decline in tobacco use among middle school students.
13 percent decline in marijuana use among middle school students.
22 percent decline in alcohol use among middle school students.
24 percent decline in alcohol use among high school students.

*Effective October 1, 2020, the DFC Program's daily management will be under the Centers for Disease Control and Prevention by agreement with ONDCP.

President Trump continues to support drug-free youth in all rural, suburban, and urban areas, especially where opioid abuse is prevalent.

Reason 71. Government Shutdown 2018/19

As the world prepared to ring in 2019, the United States federal government shut down on December 22, 2018, and would not open again until January 25, 2019. At stake, in Congress, was the public outcry for DACA mercy. For President Trump, it was funding for the U.S.-Mexico border wall. While the insults and blame-laying flew amid New Year's Eve confetti and snowflakes, government workers were furloughed—with pay, although sometimes delayed—President Trump waited at the White House to resume negotiations as the 115th U.S. Congress went on holiday. Officially, the reason for stalled negotiations was funding the federal government operation for fiscal year 2019, but the topic receiving media attention was DACA recipients.

As semantics sliced wording into "wall" and "barrier" nuances and DACA recipients were held up as protest slogans, President Trump waited to reopen talks.

This marked the longest U.S. government shutdown to date.

While Christmas, Hanukkah, Kwanzaa, and the New Year were usually times of holiday parties, family visits, and personal reflection over the past year and planning for the year ahead, President Trump remained in the people's house, the White House, dedicated to duty.

Reason 72. Supporting Law Enforcement

President Trump supports police officers and first responders. In March 2017, President Trump listened to representatives from police organizations, including, at that time, Chuck Canterbury (National President of Fraternal Order of Police), Jay McDonald (Vice President of the National Fraternal Order of Police, Ohio), Tom Penoza (Treasurer of the National

Fraternal Order of Police, Delaware), Patrick Yoes (National Secretary, Louisiana), Roger Mayberry (National Sergeant at Arms, California), and Jim Pasco (Executive Director of the National FOP, Maryland). President Trump followed up in August 2017, by approving H.R. 3298 / Public Law No. 115–45 Wounded Officers Recovery Act of 2017.

President Trump continued to salute fallen Americans in January 2019, by approving H.R. 6287 / Public Law No. 115–413 9/11 Memorial Act. This instructs the Department of the Interior to continue operating, securing, and maintaining onsite memorials regarding the September 11, 2001, terrorist attacks on the World Trade Center and Pentagon. (Sponsored by Representative Thomas MacArthur, R-NJ.)

In April 2019, President Trump approved S. 998 / Public Law No. 116–32 Supporting and Treating Officers In Crisis Act of 2019, and in July approved H.R. 1327 / Public Law No. 116–34 Never Forget the Heroes: James Zadroga, Ray Pfeifer, and Luis Alvarez Permanent Authorization of the September 11th Victim Compensation Fund Act, authorizing the latter to be funded through fiscal year 2092.

President Trump encourages positive community and police interaction, helping communities remain safe while police officers fulfill their protective duties. In October 2019, President Trump signed Executive Order EO 13896, establishing the Presidential Commission on Law Enforcement and the Administration of Justice. He followed this up in June 2020 with Executive Order 13929-Safe Policing for Safe Communities and revitalizing Project Safe Neighborhoods (PSN) to prompt communities and their local police to work with faith groups and community organizations.

Numerous police organizations support President Trump's re-election for 2020, including the Fraternal Order of Police (FOP), the nation's largest police union.

Reason 73. Pardons, Commutations & Clemencies

While most presidents wait until their last year in office (or term) to pardon prisoners or grant commutations and clemencies, President Trump acted earlier, in many cases, and after studying the crimes, offered compassion in several distinct cases.

On August 25, 2017, President Trump pardoned Joe Arpaio, former long-time sheriff of Maricopa County, Arizona. On April 13, 2018, he granted clemency to I. "Scooter" Lewis Libby, former Chief of Staff to Vice President Richard Cheney, regarding convictions coming from a 2007 trial (President George W. Bush had commuted Libby's sentence after his conviction after being fined and making other reparations).

On May 24, 2018, President Trump pardoned John Arthur "Jack" Johnson. This was followed a week later on May 31, 2018, when he granted clemency to Dinesh D'Souza (author, lecturer and filmmaker).

On May 6, 2019, President Trump also granted clemency to former Army First Lieutenant Michael Behenna of Oklahoma. The following July, President Trump gave full pardons to John Richard Bubala, Roy Wayne McKeever, Rodney Takumi, Michael Tedesco, and Chalmer Lee Williams. In February 2020, President Trump granted full pardons to Edward DeBartolo, Jr., Michael Milken, Ariel Friedler, Bernard Kerik, Paul Pogue, David Safavian, and Angela Stanton. Additionally, President Trump granted commutations to Rod Blagojevich, Tynice Nichole Hall, Crystal Munoz, and Judith Negron.

On August 18, 2020, President Trump pardoned women's suffrage advocate Susan B. Anthony (posthumously). Ten days later, President Trump fully pardoned Alice Marie Johnson (this came after commuting her life sentence in August 2018). Alice Marie Johnson became the face of prison reform and the First Step Act.

Another was Patrick J. Nolan. Nolan, a former Minority Leader of the California State Assembly (who had helped organize religious-study groups while in prison) was granted clemency on May 15, 2019. Upon his release, Nolan helped to secure the passage of several major criminal justice reforms, including the Prison Rape Elimination Act, the Second Chance Act, the Fair Sentencing Act, and the First Step Act. He is also the author of *When Prisoners Return*, a guide for churches and community groups working to help former prisoners return to communities.

Of course, Thanksgiving turkeys Peas and Carrots, Bread and Butter, and two other turkeys remaining unnamed, were pardoned from the White House dinner table.

Reason 74. Return of Prisoners and POW Remains

President Trump negotiated the release and return of Otto Warmbier, a 22-year-old student taken prisoner in North Korea. Warmbier returned to his family in a comatose state, and died in a week, shocking and saddening Americans. In June 2017, President Trump stated at a press conference that his administration would work "to prevent such tragedies from befalling innocent people at the hands of regimes that do not respect the rule of law or basic human decency. The United States once again condemns the brutality of the North Korean regime".

Ahead of President Trump's June meeting with North Korean Supreme Leader Kim Jong-un in the spring of 2018, three American prisoners, Kim Dong-chul, Tony Kim, and Kim Hak-song, were freed and returned to the U.S. President Trump met the former detainees at Joint Base Andrews with Secretary of State Mike Pompeo, who was instrumental in achieving the men's release. The former prisoners next went to Walter Reed National Military Medical Center for physical examinations.

The return of these three men was in stark contrast to the June 12, 2017, return of Otto Warmbier.

During President Trump and Kim Jong-un's June 2018 summit, North Korea reaffirmed its commitment for complete denuclearization, agreed to help the United States recover POW/MIA remains, and committed to destroying a missile engine testing site.

Under President Trump's watch, former missionary Josh Holt obtained his release from a Venezuela prison in May 2018, after being held for two years on charges of alleged spying.

Freedom was also restored for Andrew Brunson. In October 2018, President Trump met with American Pastor Andrew Brunson, a missionary to Turkey, who was detained for the last two years in the Muslim country over allegations of terrorism charges. Brunson was a Christian missionary for two decades in Turkey, and was arrested in 2016. President Trump interceded on his behalf and negotiated his release, including pressing sanctions against Turkey. Upon his return to the U.S., Brunson prayed with President Trump and for the direction of the country.

President Trump continues to seek the release and return of Americans held in foreign countries.

Reason 75. Standing up for the U.S. at the UN

On December 3, 2017, President Trump notified the United Nations the U.S. would no longer participate in the Declaration for Refugees and Migrants—which flouted the U.S. immigration policy—arranged by President Obama in September 2016.

While addressing the United Nations General Assembly in New York in September 2019, President Trump made it clear the United States was no longer the open border nation of the past. He stated plainly: "The U.S., we have taken very unprecedented action to stop the flow of illegal immigration. To anyone considering crossings of our border illegally, please hear these words: Do not pay the smugglers. Do not pay the coyotes. Do not put yourself in danger. Do not put your children in danger. Because if you make it here, you will not be allowed in; you will be promptly returned home. You will not be released into our country. As long as I am President of the United States, we will enforce our laws and protect our borders."

On September 22, 2020, President addressed the United Nations General Assembly and minced no words when speaking about the origins of the Coronavirus that impacted the world in 2020. He clearly laid the origins at the feet of the Chinese government, and then detailed the actions that downplayed the seriousness of the virus. He included the Chinese government's minimizing of the virus and contradictory or false information through the World Health Organization (WHO), while locking down its people, disallowing travel out of Wuhan, and securing medical equipment and protective supplies even as it permitted flights to leave China (after the Chinese New Year festivities), which spread the virus to the world.

President Trump called for the United Nations to hold China accountable for their actions.

He concluded with an America First message, but also for the leaders of other nations to keep their countries safe: "For decades, the same tired voices proposed the same failed solutions, pursuing global ambitions at the expense of their own people. But only when you take care of your own citizens will you find a true basis for cooperation. As President, I have rejected the failed approaches of the past, and I am proudly putting America first, just as you should be putting your countries first. That's okay—that's what you should be doing."

Reason 76. Renewable Energy

President Trump believes in harnessing natural power. In August 2020, President Trump approved several bills allowing states more time for construction of hydroelectric projects to supply local regions with clean, renewable energy. In September 2018, President Trump approved H.R. 589 / Public Law No. 115–246 Department of Energy Research and Innovation Act. This allowed the Department of Energy to seek innovations that provide clean, affordable, and reliable energy; promote economic growth; are critical for energy security; and are sustainable without government support (sponsored by Representative Lamar Smith, R-TX).

President Trump also supports the science behind safe nuclear energy. He approved S. 97 / Public Law No. 115–248 Nuclear Energy Innovation Capabilities Act of 2017 in September 2018. This allowed for scientific advances, safety analysis, and research to allow progress, enlisting experts from academia, the National Laboratories, and the private sector, enabling them to make scientific discoveries in the fields of nuclear, chemical, and materials science engineering. This also allowed for a database to store and share information in nuclear science and engineering among federal agencies and the private sector (sponsored by Senator Mike Crapo, R-ID).

Reason 77. Banks Give Back

As 2017 came to a close and the Republican tax bill was sent to President Trump's desk for signing, goodwill spread across America, and banks took notice. Hope for a better future came in generous bonuses and increased wages. Bank of America took action by giving $1,000 to its employees making up to $150,000 yearly. Texas Capital Bank spread the goodwill in late 2017 with $1,000 bonus to most employees. JPMorgan Chase announced a five-year, $20 billion investment that would include an increase in wages averaging ten percent nationwide for its 22,000 employees, expand U.S. markets, plus an uptick in small business lending by $4 billion, and adding 4,000 jobs, among other community efforts.

Reason 78. Foreign Investing in U.S.

Despite the outcry during the 2016 election about Candidate Trump wanting American isolationism, President Trump's reaching out to South Korea resulted in warm cooperation.

In November 2017, Lotte Chemical, Hankook Tire, and other South Korean companies announced plans to build production lines in southern U.S. states. This was part of a 42-company push to invest $17 billion in the U.S. by 2021. Lotte Chemical would invest $3.1 billion in a petrochemical facility in Louisiana, and Hankook Tire would build a new factory in Clarksville, Tennessee, adding $800 million into the economy. SK Innovation would begin to produce ethylene acrylic acid in Texas after acquiring Dow Chemical's EAA business for $370 million. These companies would add up to 52,000 jobs in the U.S.

With President Trump's diplomatic outreach, Masayoshi Son of SoftBank from Japan agreed to invest $50 billion dollars in the U.S., bringing in 50,000 jobs.

Reason 79. Small Businesses

President Trump supported small businesses by approving H.R. 2333 / Public Law No. 115–187 Small Business Investment Opportunity Act of 2017. This amended the Small Business Investment Act of 1958 by increasing borrowing power available to any licensed small business investment company from $150 million to $175 million (sponsored by Representative Stephen Knight, R-CA).

At the end of October 2018, President Trump also approved H.R. 6758 / Public Law No. 115–273 Study of Underrepresented Classes Chasing Engineering and Science Success Act of 2018. This later became the SUCCESS Act, which directed the U.S. Patent and Trademark Office to consult with the Small Business Administration to study and identify the best practices to potentially award more patents for underrepresented individuals.

Reason 80. The WTO

President Trump called out the imbalanced trade among "developing" countries at the World Trade Organization (WTO). The Trump Administration decided to look further into this status, evaluate it, and determined, "WTO continues to rest on an outdated dichotomy between developed and developing countries that has allowed some WTO Members to gain unfair advantages in the international trade arena. Nearly two-thirds of WTO Members have been able to avail themselves of special treatment and to take on weaker commitments under the WTO framework by designating themselves as developing countries."

With a trade deficit of over $500 billion *not* favoring the United States, in March 2017, President Trump ordered the Omnibus Report to discover where and how to remedy this imbalance (Executive Order EO 13786-Omnibus Report on Significant Trade Deficits). To ensure trade was kept favorable to the U.S., President Trump signed Executive Order EO 13797-Establishment of Office of Trade and Manufacturing Policy in April 2017. This established the Office of Trade and Manufacturing Policy (OTMP) within the White House Office. The OTMP's mission was "to defend and serve American workers and domestic manufacturers while advising the
100

President on policies to increase economic growth, decrease the trade deficit, and strengthen the United States manufacturing and defense industrial bases." It also served to advise the President on innovative strategies and promote the President's trade policies in accordance with those described in Executive Order EO 13788 of April 18, 2017 (Buy American and Hire American).

President Trump also requested details about China's compliance with the WTO commitments (August 2020) and Russia's implementation of its WTO commitments (August 2020).

President Trump pushed for a renewed effort to follow the Buy-American Act guidance in seeking American-made goods and products made from American materials first to keep Americans working and prosperous (reaffirming the Executive Order 10582 of Dec. 17, 1954).

Reason 81. Stock Market Soars

Stock markets shot up with the prospect of Donald Trump taking office. By January 25, 2017, stock gains topped $2 trillion in wealth since President Trump was elected.

From the time President Trump won the election on November 8, 2016, the DJIA went from 18251.38 to 24719.22 on the last day of business for 2017. This would increase nearly 5000 during President Trump's first eleven months in office (the DJIA would continue to steadily climb, closing over 25000 on January 4, 2018, for the first time ever, within President Trump's first full year in office). This broke records across the field.

Before COVID-19 officially reached America's shores and President Trump declared a national emergency and made the decision to close the borders to travel from China, the DJIA had reached over 29398 in February 2020. After the full brunt of COVID-19 impact, the markets dropped to 19173.98 on March 18, 2020, wiping out the gains of years in a massive sell off. The future looked uncertain.

As President Trump assured Americans they would get through this time together, and Vice President Pence and the Coronavirus Task Force put into place precautions, the markets adjusted. President Trump was looking out for Americans with supplemental incomes, and for their jobs with Paycheck Protection Program that enabled businesses to keep employees on payroll and the workforce ready. As a result, the market did not collapse completely, and rolled back to full force in June 2020 at 27110. By August 25, 2020, it had reached near highs with 28653.

Within months, the markets were back in full swing. Employment, after rising to an unemployment high of 14.7% (the highest since 1948, losing over 700,000 jobs in March 2020) rebounded by September 2020, with unemployment dropping to 8.4, similar to where the unemployment rate was in December 2011 and January 2012 (8.5 and 8.3 respectively), under President Obama.

Under President Trump's direction, the American economy was roaring back.

Reason 82. Opportunity Zones

Following the GOP tax bill, the Tax Cuts and Jobs Act that President Trump had signed in December 2017, the Trump Administration created Opportunity Zones (OZ) to serve business and entrepreneurial needs in economically stressed areas. These sections of low-income areas were chosen from blocks nominated by each state (some approved were as few as 20 sites (NE), or as many as 169 sites (NJ)). The move was greeted with great support by policy makers, governors, and state leaders and officials, including Senate Majority Leader Mitch McConnell (R-KY), Sen. Rand Paul (R-KY), Sen. Deb Fischer (R-NE), Sen. Ben Sasse (R-NE), Oklahoma Native American Affairs Secretary Chris Benge, Nebraska Department of Economic Development Director Dave Rippe, Oklahoma Native American Affairs Secretary Chris Benge, Mississippi Development Authority Executive Director Glenn McCullough, Jr., Idaho Department of Commerce Director Bobbi-Jo Meuleman, Colorado Department of Local Affairs Executive Director Irv Halter, Governor Kenneth Mapp (I-VI), Governor Mary Fallin (R-OK), Governor Phil Murphy (D-NJ), Governor Rick Snyder (R-MI), Governor Matt Bevin (R-KY), Governor C.L. "Butch" Otter (R-ID), Governor John Hickenlooper (D-CO), and Governor Doug Ducey (R-AZ).

These OZs opened up more opportunity to under-served areas not typically attracting business or entrepreneurial activity, such as a new timber plant in the San Luis Valley, Colorado or an agriculture processing plant for the Eastern Plains (also Colorado); rising wages and worker bonuses in Nebraska; addressing rebuilding rural and urban areas on the Mississippi River in West Kentucky, throughout neighborhoods in West Louisville, and deep in Appalachia; urban, rural, and tribal areas in Wisconsin; rebuilding after hurricanes in the Virgin Islands; tribal nations; and other commercial, industrial, housing, infrastructure and other investment projects. Funds could also be used to rebuild homes, schools, businesses, and communities.

As of September 2020, 8,764 Opportunity Zones stretched across the United States, with some in U.S. overseas territories and Washington DC.

Reason 83. Protecting Intellectual Property

In mid-August 2017, President Trump signed a Memorandum on Addressing China's Laws, Policies, Practices, and Actions

Related to Intellectual Property, Innovation, and Technology. This would stem violations of intellectual property rights (and other unfair technology transfers) that may threaten the U.S. and undermine fair play in the global market. After this investigation found China using various methods to pressure technology transfers from U.S. companies to Chinese entities and administrative reviews and licensing procedures to transfers to weaken the U.S.'s global competitiveness, and other means of "stealing" IP, President Trump signed Actions by the United States Related to the Section 301 Investigation of China's Laws, Policies, Practices, or Actions Related to Technology Transfer, Intellectual Property, and Innovation in March 2018.

According to a Council of Economic Advisers (CEA) 2018 report, malicious cyber activity and IP infringement cost the U.S. economy between $57 billion and $109 billion in 2016 (for example, an attack by Chinese hackers on SolarWorld AG based in Germany, showcased the impact of IP theft).

Not seeing enough action on China's part to adhere to the IP rights security, in April 2019, President Trump signed a Memorandum on Combating Trafficking in Counterfeit and Pirated Goods, and on January 31, 2020, signed Executive Order EO 13904-Ensuring Safe and Lawful E-Commerce for United States Consumers, Businesses, Government Supply Chains, and Intellectual Property Rights.

Reason 84. Companies Invest in U.S.

After running a campaign promoting Made in America and bringing jobs back to the U.S., President Trump's persuasiveness paid off for American workers. One of these companies was Ford, who rerouted a planned Mexico plant to Flat Rock, Michigan, adding 700 U.S. jobs and $700 million in investment. In February 2017, Intel announced it would invest $7 billion to build a factory in Arizona, creating about 3,000 jobs. Later in March 2017, Charter Communications committed to invest $25 billion in the U.S. and to hire 20,000 American workers over the next four years. Charter would also invest $17 million to open a new Spanish-language call center in McAllen, Texas, and hire more than 600 workers.

Going into 2018, Toyota Motor announced a $10 billion investment plan in the U.S. over the next five years. In January 2108, Apple took a big bite into the U.S. market—stateside, announcing plans to invest in excess of $30 billion in the U.S. over the next five years. Included in this was $1 to $5 billion in U.S. manufacturing companies and the domestic manufacturing sector. This was expected to create 20,000 new jobs.

Reason 85. Companies Expand Across U.S.

On September 7, 2017, with President Trump's plans to bring back American jobs and the new income that would bring, Amazon.com announced plans to open a massive second headquarters to expand distribution. Plans included investing $5 billion in construction and hiring 50,000 full-time employees. This would later be something Americans needed during 2020's COVID-19 pandemic.

Under the new GOP tax relief law of 2017, low-cost grocery store chain Aldi planned to add 180 new stores.

With the new surge in dollars available in paychecks, Dollar General planned to open 900 new brick-and-mortar stores in 2018 nationwide and remodel stores at 1,000 locations. The company also planned to open of a distribution center in Longview, Texas, creating about 400 new jobs.

In January 2018, biopharma giant Amgen CEO Robert Bradway announced plans to add 1,600 new jobs to U.S. manufacturing. This was up from a 15 percent cut in workforce and the closing of two manufacturing plants in 2014 in cost-saving measures.

With President Trump's plans for cutting taxes (which happened with the GOP tax bill in late 2017), besides Dollar General's 900 new stores, Dollar Tree and Family Dollar planned to add over 300 stores each.

Reason 86. Renewed Confidence in U.S. Industry

As President Trump took office in 2017, manufacturing confidence hit record highs as Americans and companies looked to a brighter future. In March 2017, 93.3 percent of the NAM Outlook Survey from respondents were positive about their company's outlook. This was an all-time high in the 20-year history of the survey. By the third-quarter survey of 2017, NAM reported the highest consecutive three-quarters average of 90.9 percent of respondents having a positive outlook for their company—highest in the survey's history.

On November 28, 2017, the Conference Board Consumer Confidence Index hit a 17-year high of 129.5. Under President Trump's job creation efforts, NAM's first-quarter report in March 2018, highlighted the continuing results of regulation-removal processes. U.S. manufacturing survey respondents gave high marks for their company's positive outlook, with Small Manufacturers at 94.5 percent, Medium-Sized Manufacturers at 93 percent, and Large Manufacturers at 93.8 percent. Overall, manufacturers expected production growth rate to rise 5.5 percent over the next twelve months. Full-time was expected to rise 2.9 percent over the same time period—an all-time high.

Employee wages were expected to rise 2.6 percent over the next twelve months, the highest since 2001. Sales were expected to grow at a rate of 5.7 percent over that time, the highest rate since 1997.

The Trump Administration apprenticeship and non-college job plans were working, too. According to NAM's survey for the second quarter for 2018, two-thirds of those surveyed stated they would increase apprenticeship, mentoring or other training over the next year. Around 90 percent of those employers claimed to train or otherwise upskill their existing employees. With manufacturing unleashed, a full 95 percent of companies in NAM's second quarter for 2018 were very positive/somewhat positive about the outlook for their company. Most respondents (76 percent) also expected an increase of 5-10 percent in profits over the next year. Most surveyed were in the fabricated metal products fields, machinery, and plastics and rubber products.

Respondents for NAM's 2018's third-quarter survey were 92.5 percent positive about the outlook for their companies, with Large Manufacturers at 93.1 percent, both reaching all-time highs. The Trump Administration's tax reform and regulatory relief efforts resulted in surveyed manufacturers continuing their unprecedented levels of optimism. The robust outlook for the economy through 2018 was a 20-year high. While employers participating in the NAM Outlook Survey for the third quarter of 2018 anticipated larger workloads and expanding floor space, finding qualified workers was still an issue. One-fourth of respondents claimed they had to turn down new business due to lack of skilled workers. Ninety-three percent expected to increase wages over the next year.

Higher consumer confidence hit in 2018. The Consumer Confidence Sentiment Index averaged 98.4 in 2018, the best since 2000. The highest was in March 2018, at 101.4, and touching again at 100.1 in September.

Just before the COVID-19 pandemic, President Trump's plan for the U.S. economy was working, and the United States Consumer Sentiment reached a 10-year high in January 2020 at 111.40.

Reason 87. Big Companies Repatriate Money to U.S.

President Trump's signing of the 2017 GOP tax bill allowed companies holding offshore funds to bring overseas cash back into the U.S. for a one-time tax holiday of lowered rates. Companies holding large amounts overseas included GE ($35 billion), Foot Locker ($1 billion), Citrix Systems ($2 billion), Western Digital ($5 billion), Waters Corp. ($3 billion), Ralph Lauren ($1 billion), Microsoft ($128 billion), Oracle ($48 billion), Amgen ($36 billion), Apple ($216 billion), Qualcomm ($30 billion), NetApp ($5 billion), and Cisco Systems ($68 billion).

American jobs came home in 2017, and some of the company names were huge. Apple reshored 22,000 jobs and paid $38 billion on profits, lower than the previous law's rate allowed. Apple repatriated $285 billion from foreign accounts.

In February 2018, in response to President Trump's economic plans, giant biopharma industry Amgen announced a $300 million investment in a new biologics plant in the U.S. This would add 300 manufacturing jobs. Later in April, Amgen stated in a press release that the location would be West Greenwich, Rhode Island.

Reason 88. Time-Honored American Companies Come Home

With President Trump signing the GOP tax bill in 2017 and the President's nudging, a retro toy came home when U.S. Hasbro Inc. announced manufacturing of Play-Doh once again in its Massachusetts factory by the end of 2018. AT&T brought 3,000 outsourced jobs back to the U.S. Boeing brought back over 7,700 jobs, and Ford and General Motors 17,000 jobs, collectively. Plans for new plants and expansions were on the drafting tables.

In early November 2017, Broadcom Limited, a $100 billion semiconductor company, announced it would officially relocate its home address from Singapore to the U.S., namely Delaware. It also promised to bring $20 billion in annual revenue back. Broadcom employed about 7,500 in the U.S. at the time. In June 2018, tariffs paid off for the U.S. as Whirlpool reshored 2,165 domestic manufacturing jobs to the U.S. Two hundred of these full-time jobs were for the Clyde, Ohio, location (Whirlpool is headquartered in Benton Harbor, Michigan). This news came after President Trump announced safeguard tariffs on selected types of imported appliances.

Reason 89. Voluntary Minimum Wage Increases

In July 2017, under President Trump's negotiating skills, Foxconn announced a plan to spend $10 billion over the next three years on a 20,000-square-foot plant in Wisconsin. This would employ up to 13,000 employees, and would be the first of several plants in the U.S. heartland.

Before the close of 2017, Wells Fargo also said it would raise its hourly minimum wage to $15, up from $13.50, and planned to donate $400 million to community and nonprofit organizations in 2018.

Spreading the wealth—voluntarily. Among those companies being generous with rewards in 2017-2018 was retail mega-store Wal-Mart. Due to recapturing costs with its new tax percentage of 21 percent rather than its previous percent, Wal-Mart voluntarily raised minimum wage for U.S. employees to $11 per hour. Wal-Mart had over one million hourly employees at the time.

As President Trump reworked the U.S. economy and eased regulations, Intel Corporation CEO Brian Krzanich announced Intel would invest over $7 billion to construct Fab 42 in

Chandler, Arizona, in early 2018. Expected to be the most-advanced semiconductor factory in the world, it was expected to be completed by 2022. It will employ 3,000 workers. Most jobs will be high-tech, engineering, technician, and support jobs.

Reason 90. Rebuilding Infrastructure

On July 19, 2017, President Trump signed Executive Order EO 13805-Establishing a Presidential Advisory Council on Infrastructure, readying America's launch into a new and productive future.

In mid-May 2017, President Trump approved S. 496 / Public Law No. 115–33 To repeal the rule issued by the Federal Highway Administration and the Federal Transit Administration entitled "Metropolitan Planning Organization Coordination and Planning Area Reform." This Act would have made MPOs consolidate or absorb surrounding areas. Repealing this Act from December 20, 2016, leaves more control to the states.

President Trump sent a Message to the Congress Transmitting a Legislative Outline for Rebuilding Infrastructure in America, requesting Congress to act shortly on an infrastructure bill of at least $1.5 trillion in new investment over the next ten years, shorten the process for approving projects to two years or less, address unmet rural infrastructure needs and allow state and local authorities to train the American workforce of the future. He asked for more than traditional infrastructure (roads, bridges, airports), but also needs like drinking and wastewater systems, waterways, water resources, energy, rural infrastructure, public lands, and veteran hospitals.

Rebuilding America's essential utilities. Part of the Trump Administration's infrastructure plans, noted in the February "Legislative Outline for Rebuilding Infrastructure in America",
110

included California's I-405 Project in Orange Country, California High-Speed Rail Project, and several other high-speed rail projects, as well as drainage, runoff, and subway projects. Other projects were slated for preconstruction phases. In August 2018, job prediction for these areas was expected to be up to 7.5 million jobs by 2026 (from 7.2 million over the previous month).

In January 2019, President Trump signed Executive Order EO 13858-Strengthening Buy-American Preferences for Infrastructure Projects; this braced the Buy-American principles in Federal financial assistance programs.

Also in January 2017, President Trump signed Executive Order EO 13766-Expediting Environmental Reviews and Approvals for High Priority Infrastructure Projects, and Executive Order EO 13807-Establishing Discipline and Accountability in the Environmental Review and Permitting Process for Infrastructure Projects in August 2017. This not only sped up permitting, but safeguarded environmental concerns for the projects.

Reason 91. U.S. Protections

President Trump took a close look at protecting Americans on personal fronts, including cyber safety, voting safety, and election integrity.

In April 2018, President Trump signed Executive Order EO 13829-Task Force on the United States Postal System, forcing the postal system to operate within their budget means and re-enable their employee obligations, protecting thousands of employees. Since the 2007-2009 recession, the USPS incurred $65 billion of cumulative losses and was since unable to make payments required by law for its retiree health benefit obligations (totaling more than $38 billion at the end of fiscal year 2017). This would later (2020 presidential election) give way to some media and politicians howling about President Trump's attempt to "slow the mail" to benefit his re-election.

On September 12, 2018, President Trump signed Executive Order EO 13848-Imposing Certain Sanctions in the Event of Foreign Interference in a United States Election. This addressed foreign interference targeting election infrastructure materially affecting the security or integrity of infrastructure, tabulation of votes, or timely transmission of election results, including alteration or falsification of information or data. This became vital as the 2020 presidential election closed in.

In November 2017, President Trump approved S. 782 / Public Law No. 115–82 Providing Resources, Officers, and Technology To Eradicate Cyber Threats to Our Children Act of 2017. This was needed in the increasing availability of the internet to users of all ages in various forms.

In August 2020, President Trump, citing national emergency aspects in respect to the information and communications technology and services supply chain declared in Executive Order EO 13873 of May 15, 2019 (Securing the Information and Communications Technology and Services Supply Chain), warned of prohibiting TikTok (video-sharing mobile app owned by Chinese company ByteDance Ltd.) from operating in the U.S.

Government agencies had already banned TikTok on Federal Government phones, and the Government of India had banned TikTok and other Chinese mobile apps, referencing the ability to steal and surreptitiously transmit user data in an unauthorized manner to servers outside India. President Trump demanded that ByteDance destroy all TikTok app or Musical.ly app data collected from U.S. users. President Trump has since given a time period for TikTok to be separated from China using an American company. At the time of this writing,

Wal-Mart, Microsoft, and Oracle were showing interest, but no decision was made.

Similarly to TikTok, President Trump has taken a closer look at messaging app WeChat, which is owned by Chinese company Tencent Holdings Ltd., with over a billion users. WeChat automatically captures large amounts of user information, which may be used for the Communist Party to spy on users. Similar actions as those taken regarding TikTok are in progress for WeChat.

President Trump continues to guard Americans' privacy, communication, and voting concerns from every angle.

Reason 92. Tech Jobs Came Back

As President Trump took office in January 2017, tech companies primed for the push for a Made in America stamp on their products. Some of that push was more of a digital label. One was IBM, which announced that not only was it canceling a planned massive layoff, but would invest $1 billion in the U.S. over the next four years and add 25,000 new U.S.-based jobs. Sprint decided to add another 5,000 U.S. jobs onto the previous 5,000 promised jobs.

Using the GOP tax bill of late 2017, Apple expected to contribute $350 billion to the U.S. economy over the next five years, would create 20,000 new jobs, planned to open a new campus, and would bring home about $38 billion in taxes (on its repatriated funds under tax reshoring).

In February 2017, Intel announced it would invest $7 billion to build a factory in Arizona, creating about 3,000 jobs.

In late March 2017, Charter Communications committed to invest $25 billion in the U.S. and hire 20,000 American workers over the next four years. Charter would also invest $17 million to open a new Spanish-language call center in McAllen, Texas, and hire more than 600 workers.

Reason 93. American Innovation

President Trump stepped up the possibilities of American innovation in March 2017 when he signed the Presidential Memorandum on The White House Office of American Innovation. In April 2017, he signed Executive Order EO 13794-Establishment of the American Technology Council, to keep America on technology forefronts. Members would include the President (who serves as Chairman), the Vice President, the Secretary of Defense, the Secretary of Commerce, the Secretary of Homeland Security, the Director of National Intelligence, the Director of the Office of Management and Budget (OMB), the Director of the Office of Science and Technology Policy, the U.S. Chief Technology Officer, and others.

In mid-August 2017, President Trump signed a Memorandum on Addressing China's Laws, Policies, Practices, and Actions Related to Intellectual Property, Innovation, and Technology. This was to look into what, if any, role China was playing in IP issues and loss of control over technology from U.S. companies. He also planned to address any unfair practices with the UN to maintain a level playing field for the U.S. American innovation was being stolen or otherwise compromised by forced transfer of core technologies in joint ventures, making certain manufacturers disclose development and manufacturing technology, and cyber intrusions into U.S. companies were accessing trade secrets. These unfair policies and practices cost U.S. companies tens of billion of dollars in damages each year.

President Trump signed Executive Order EO 13859-Maintaining American Leadership in Artificial Intelligence in February 2019, to position America at the forefront of AI possibilities. He championed further innovation in farming and agricultural biotechnology in June 2019 with the signing of Executive Order EO 13874-Modernizing the Regulatory Framework for Agricultural Biotechnology Products, enabling U.S. farmers to feed America, and much of the world.

Reason 94. Less Need for Public Assistance

When President Trump took office in 2017, December 2016 Supplemental Nutrition Assistance Program (SNAP) needs were 42,972,692 persons and 21,232,456 households. Costs for FY2017 were $63,711,050,937.

As President Trump's job creation measures, including the GOP tax bill of 2017, reshoring of U.S. companies and jobs, and the repatriation of funds by companies (especially big tech and the connected lower tax rates) took hold, the economy lifted and headed into an upward direction. By the end of 2019, SNAP needs were 35,702,611 persons and 17,964,076 households, costing $55,621,882,213 (FY2019).

SNAP dependency rose with the onset of nationwide COVID-19 lockdowns, but began the V-shaped recovery through the summer of 2020. President Trump's Paycheck Protection Program measures and state reopenings allowed hastening of the post-Coronavirus rebound.

Reason 95. Space Force

President Trump created the U.S.'s sixth military branch. In mid-December 2017, President Trump signed a Presidential Memorandum on Reinvigorating America's Human Space

Exploration Program, and Executive Order EO 13803 of June 30, 2017-Reviving the National Space Council. These set the groundwork for the future Space Force. This was followed by five directives (as of September 2020):

Space Policy Directive-1 Reinvigorating America's Human Space Exploration Program
Space Policy Directive-2 Streamlining Regulations on Commercial Use of Space
Space Policy Directive-3 National Space Traffic Management Policy
Space Policy Directive-4 Establishment of the United States Space Force
Space Policy Directive-5 Cybersecurity Principles for Space Systems

With President Trump's vision for protecting America, this program continues to develop a new approach to space traffic management (STM), and when combined with other legislature, opens the door wide for women in space and astronauts landing on Mars. It is designed to lessen current and future risks through government and commercial expertise, and lets the U.S. become independent of relying foreign governments.

Reason 96. JFK Transparency

President Trump allowed JFK Assassination Documents to be made public on October 26, 2017. This was the first time many of these pages were allowed viewing by the public. The National Archives released 3,539 documents on Dec. 15; 10,744 documents on Nov. 17; 13,213 documents on Nov. 9; 676 documents on Nov. 3; and the final 19,045 documents released on April 26, 2018.

Reason 97. Solid Stability

On May 9, 2017, less than six months into his first year in office, President Trump signed a Letter to Federal Bureau of Investigation Director James B. Comey, Jr., Informing Him of His Termination and Removal From Office. This set off a series of events that occupied the next three years, many times hampering President Trump's ability to easily govern, yet still President Trump governed, steadily pushing forward his America First agenda.

On May 17, 2017, President Trump signed a Statement on the Appointment of Former Federal Bureau of Investigation Director Robert S. Mueller III as Special Counsel To Oversee the Investigation of Russian Government Efforts To Influence the 2016 Presidential Election and Related Matters. This set in motion repercussions that would impact his first administrative term.

President Trump approved S. 2896 / Public Law No. 115–418 Justice Against Corruption on K Street Act of 2018 (or the JACK Act). This bill required each lobbyist registration and lobbying quarterly report to include dates of conviction and description of offenses of any listed lobbyist convicted of an offense involving bribery, extortion, embezzlement, illegal kickback, tax evasion, fraud, conflict of interest, making a false statement, perjury, or money laundering. (Sponsored by John Kennedy, R-LA.)

While the Mueller team investigated President Trump and many people in his orbit, President Trump continued to govern, lowering taxes, bringing jobs back to the U.S., seating Supreme Court Justices, negotiating fair trade deals, and making America great again. And as 2019 came to a close and his political opponents ran the House of Representatives, impeachment clouded President Trump's third year and into his fourth. After Mueller's Special Counsel Investigation and following hearings gave no credence for crimes, the House held hidden meetings that dissolved into full impeachment as 2019 changed into 2020. House Speaker Pelosi was still hesitating to send the Articles of Impeachment to the Senate in January 2020 as the Coronavirus was quietly seeping into American cities.

And despite being called a racist and tyrant for closing air travel to the U.S. from China and vilified as seeking a distraction from his impeachment in the House of Representatives, President Trump safeguarded the American public from further exposure to the Coronavirus. His acquittal in the Senate was solid, even as a new danger rose before the American people.

The world took notice of President Trump's hard work during all this, too. President Trump was nominated for the 2020 Nobel Peace Prize by the Norwegian Parliament for his role in brokering the Abraham Accords peace deal between Israel, Bahrain, and the United Arab Emirates in 2020. Several days later, President Trump received his second nomination, this from Magnus Jacobsson of the Swedish Parliament, for his work in the Serbia and Kosovo peace negotiations in 2020. As September 2020 came to a close, President Trump received his third Nobel Peace Prize nomination, this time from a group of Australian law professors for the Trump Doctrine, President Trump's policy of getting America out and staying out of futile and endless wars.

Reason 98. The Trump 2020 Second Term Agenda

President Trump has a plan for the future of the United States, including a post-Coronavirus nation. His agenda includes:

Create 10 Million New Jobs in 10 Months
Create 1 Million New Small Businesses

Cut Taxes to Boost Take-Home Pay and Keep Jobs in America
Enact Fair Trade Deals that Protect American Jobs
"Made in America" Tax Credits
Expand Opportunity Zones
Continue Deregulatory Agenda for Energy Independence
Develop a COVID0-19 Vaccine by the End Of 2020
Return to Normal in 2021
Make All Critical Medicines and Supplies for Healthcare Workers in the United States
Refill Stockpiles and Prepare for Future Pandemics
End U.S. Reliance on China
Bring Back 1 Million Manufacturing Jobs from China
Tax Credits for Companies that Bring Back Jobs from China
Allow 100% Expensing Deductions for Essential Industries like Pharmaceuticals and Robotics who Bring Back their Manufacturing to the United States
No Federal Contracts for Companies who Outsource to China
Hold China Fully Accountable for Allowing the Virus to Spread around the World
Cut Prescription Drug Prices
Put Patients and Doctors Back in Charge of our Healthcare System
Lower Healthcare Insurance Premiums
End Surprise Billing
Cover All Pre-Existing Conditions
Protect Social Security and Medicare
Protect Our Veterans and Provide World-Class Healthcare and Services
Provide School Choice to Every Child in America
Teach American Exceptionalism
Pass Congressional Term Limits
End Bureaucratic Government Bullying of U.S. Citizens and Small Businesses
Expose Washington's Money Trail and Delegate Powers Back to People and States
Drain the Globalist Swamp by Taking on International Organizations That Hurt American Citizens

Fully Fund and Hire More Police and Law Enforcement Officers

Increase Criminal Penalties for Assaults on Law Enforcement Officers

Prosecute Drive-By Shootings as Acts of Domestic Terrorism

Bring Violent Extremist Groups Like ANTIFA to Justice

End Cashless Bail and Keep Dangerous Criminals Locked Up until Trial

Block Illegal Immigrants from Becoming Eligible for Taxpayer-Funded Welfare, Healthcare, and Free College Tuition

Mandatory Deportation for Non-Citizen Gang Members

Dismantle Human Trafficking Networks

End Sanctuary Cities to Restore our Neighborhoods and Protect our Families

Prohibit American Companies from Replacing United States Citizens with Lower-Cost Foreign Workers

Require New Immigrants to Be Able to Support Themselves Financially

Launch Space Force, Establish Permanent Manned Presence on The Moon and Send the First Manned Mission to Mars

Build the World's Greatest Infrastructure System

Win the Race to 5G and Establish a National High-Speed Wireless Internet Network

Continue to Lead the World in Access to the Cleanest Drinking Water and Cleanest Air

Partner with Other Nations to Clean Up our Planet's Oceans

America First Foreign Policy

Stop Endless Wars and Bring Our Troops Home

Get Allies to Pay their Fair Share

Maintain and Expand America's Unrivaled Military Strength

Wipe Out Global Terrorists Who Threaten to Harm Americans

Build a Great Cybersecurity Defense System and Missile Defense System

Defend American Values

Continue nominating constitutionalist Supreme Court and lower court judges

Protect unborn life through every means available

120

Defend the freedoms of religious believers and organizations
Support the exercise of Second Amendment rights

Reason 99. President Trump Does it for (Almost) Free

President Trump ran his 2016 campaign with the claim to be president for free—taking no salary. However, since 3 U.S. Code § 102 requires U.S. presidents to be paid a salary, President Trump agreed to a $1.00 salary. The rest of his salary President Trump donates to a variety of causes and charities.

Here is where President Trump donated his quarterly salary of $100,000 (through second-quarter 2020).

2017 Quarter 1: President Trump, who has never accepted his salary as personal payment (save the mandatory amount of $1.00), donated his first-quarter presidential salary to the National Park Service, which will go toward restoring two projects at a national battlefield.
2017 Quarter 2: Department of Education. The funds will be used to host a Science, Technology, Engineering, and Math (STEM)-focused camp for students.
2017 Quarter 3: Department of Health and Human Services for public awareness campaign about opioid addiction.
2017 Quarter 4: Department of Transportation for the department's INFRA (Infrastructure For Rebuilding America) Grant Programs.

2018 Quarter 1: Department of Veterans Affairs to support caregiver programs.
2018 Quarter 2: U.S. Small Business Administration for the Emerging Leaders program.
2018 Quarter 3: National Institute on Alcohol Abuse and Alcoholism
2018 Quarter 4: Department of Homeland Security

2019 Quarter 1: Department of Agriculture outreach programs
2019 Quarter 2: Surgeon General's Office
2019 Quarter 3: Office of the Assistant Secretary of Health to battle the opioid crisis.
2019 Quarter 4: Department of Health and Human Services, to confront, contain, and combat COVID-19.

2020 Quarter 1: Department of Health and Human Services, to develop new therapies for treating and preventing Coronavirus.
2020 Quarter 2: National Park Service for the restoration of America's national monuments.

Reason 100. President Trump Believes in America

Donald Trump believes in America and its citizens, which is why he ran for president when he saw the unfair trade deals, disadvantageous taxes that sent U.S. companies offshore, and the steady decline of American incomes, lifestyle, and confidence. At the close of the eight-year run of the Obama Administration, America needed a cheerleader who saw its potential again and extended a hand to lift it up. Candidate Trump offered bright hope, not a constant barrage of *you didn't build that*, where dropping wages and miniscule job growth were the new normal as jobs fled the U.S., and citizens were pressed with increasingly burdensome regulations and stifling political correctness. (Remember, the September 2020 COVID-10 rebound unemployment rate of 8.4—almost double what it had been in January 2020—was the "new normal" unemployment rate under the Obama Administration in December 2011-January 2012 (8.5 and 8.3) because *those jobs weren't coming back*.) President Trump put the focus on the American people rather than punish them for globalist interests.

President Trump represented a change, a return to cooperation between all Americans, not divisiveness by color or life choices fostered by media, social platforms, and a few very vocal spokespeople. President Trump's tax reform, VA agenda, apprenticeship programs, COVID-19 response, and America-First Healthcare Plan benefit all Americans, not just his supporters. President Trump didn't let the R or D in a politician's title get in the way of sound legislation. A good idea was a good idea. It didn't matter which side of the aisle brought it to his desk.

Early in his presidency, on February 28, 2017, in an address to Congress, President Trump stated: "From now on, America will be empowered by our aspirations, not burdened by our fears; inspired by the future, not bound by the failures of the past; and guided by our vision, not blinded by our doubts." This was long before the city burnings, the riots and hijacked protests, and the removal of historic symbols.

More than ever, America needs a president who believes in its people.

Reason 101. WINNING: The Art of National Recovery

President Trump goes past trying and actually *does*. He doesn't merely attempt, he succeeds. President Trump does not stop at talking about a challenge; he tackles and overcomes the challenge. Just look at the jobs coming back to America, the expanding jobs market, the lowering unemployment and record job numbers for Black and African Americans, women, Hispanics, and every other category of worker.

President Trump is a good steward of the United States voters entrusted him to safeguard. President Trump is a proven strategist and peacemaker, and he represents strength. He has already turned around a failing, flailing American economy before the COVID-19 outbreak.

And he can enable the American people to do it again.

In the past, most U.S. leaders were, as the Motor City would have put it, all show and no go. All talk and no walk.

Past presidents made promises. President Trump delivers success.

Your Reasons:

Sources

2021 Note: Sources may be found at the President Trump Administration Archives
https://www.archives.gov/presidential-libraries/archived-websites
https://trumpwhitehouse.archives.gov/

Reason 1. President Trump Listens

Readout of the White House Historically Black Colleges & Universities (HBCUs) Leadership Listening Session
https://trumpwhitehouse.archives.gov/briefings-statements/readout-white-house-historically-black-colleges-universities-hbcus-leadership-listening-session/

Remarks by President Trump in African American History Month Listening Session
https://www.trumpwhitehouse.archives.gov/briefings-statements/remarks-president-trump-african-american-history-month-listening-session/

Remarks by President Trump in Listening Session with the Retail Industry Leaders Association and Member Company CEOs
https://trumpwhitehouse.archives.gov/briefings-statements/remarks-president-trump-listening-session-retail-industry-leaders-association-member-company-ceos/

Remarks by President Trump at Listening Session on Domestic and International Human Trafficking
https://trumpwhitehouse.archives.gov/briefings-statements/remarks-president-trump-listening-session-domestic-international-human-trafficking/

Remarks by President Trump at Parent-Teacher Conference Listening Session
https://trumpwhitehouse.archives.gov/briefings-statements/remarks-president-trump-parent-teacher-conference-listening-session/

Remarks by President Trump in Listening Session with Health Insurance Company CEOs
https://trumpwhitehouse.archives.gov/briefings-statements/remarks-president-trump-listening-session-health-insurance-company-ceos/

Remarks by President Trump in Parent-Teacher Conference Listening Session
https://trumpwhitehouse.archives.gov/briefings-statements/remarks-president-trump-parent-teacher-conference-listening-session-2/

Remarks by President Trump in Listening Session with the Fraternal Order of Police
https://trumpwhitehouse.archives.gov/briefings-statements/remarks-president-trump-listening-session-fraternal-order-police/

Remarks by President Trump in Listening Session on Opioids and Drug Abuse
https://trumpwhitehouse.archives.gov/briefings-statements/remarks-president-trump-listening-session-opioids-drug-abuse/

Remarks by President Trump and Veterans Affairs Secretary Shulkin at Veterans Affairs Listening Session
https://trumpwhitehouse.archives.gov/briefings-statements/remarks-president-trump-veterans-affairs-secretary-shulkin-veterans-affairs-listening-session/

Readout of President Donald J. Trump's National Economic Council Listening Session
https://trumpwhitehouse.archives.gov/briefings-statements/readout-president-donald-j-trumps-national-economic-council-listening-session/

Remarks by President Trump in National Economic Council Listening Session with CEOs of Small and Community Banks
https://trumpwhitehouse.archives.gov/briefings-statements/remarks-president-trump-national-economic-council-listening-session-ceos-small-community-banks/

Remarks by the Vice President in a Listening Session with Small Business Owners
https://trumpwhitehouse.archives.gov/briefings-statements/remarks-vice-president-listening-session-small-business-owners/

Agriculture Tax Reform Listening Session
https://trumpwhitehouse.archives.gov/articles/agriculture-tax-reform-listening-session/

Remarks by President Trump at Working Session with Mayors
https://trumpwhitehouse.archives.gov/briefings-statements/remarks-president-trump-working-session-mayors/

Remarks by President Trump in Listening Session with Representatives from the Steel and Aluminum Industry
https://trumpwhitehouse.archives.gov/briefings-statements/remarks-president-trump-listening-session-representatives-steel-aluminum-industry/

Remarks by President Trump in a Listening Session on Youth Vaping and the Electronic Cigarette Epidemic
https://trumpwhitehouse.archives.gov/briefings-statements/remarks-president-trump-listening-session-youth-vaping-electronic-cigarette-epidemic/

Made in America Roundtable
https://trumpwhitehouse.archives.gov/articles/made-america-
roundtable/

*President Trump Hosts Tribal, State, and Local Energy
Roundtable*
https://trumpwhitehouse.archives.gov/articles/president-trump-
hosts-tribal-state-local-energy-roundtable/

*Remarks by President Trump at National Sheriffs' Association
Roundtable*
https://trumpwhitehouse.archives.gov/briefings-
statements/remarks-president-trump-national-sheriffs-
association-roundtable/

*Remarks by President Trump at Customs and Border
Protection Roundtable*
https://trumpwhitehouse.archives.gov/briefings-
statements/remarks-president-trump-customs-border-
protection-roundtable/

*Remarks by President Trump at a California Sanctuary State
Roundtable*
https://trumpwhitehouse.archives.gov/briefings-
statements/remarks-president-trump-california-sanctuary-state-
roundtable/

*Remarks by President Trump at a Roundtable with Automaker
CEOs*
https://trumpwhitehouse.archives.gov/briefings-
statements/remarks-president-trump-roundtable-automaker-
ceos/

*Remarks by President Trump at Protecting American Workers
Roundtable*
https://trumpwhitehouse.archives.gov/briefings-
statements/remarks-president-trump-protecting-american-
workers-roundtable/

Remarks by President Trump at Workforce Development Roundtable
https://trumpwhitehouse.archives.gov/briefings-statements/remarks-president-trump-workforce-development-roundtable/

Remarks by President Trump at Prison Reform Roundtable
https://trumpwhitehouse.archives.gov/briefings-statements/remarks-president-trump-prison-reform-roundtable/

Remarks by President Trump at Defense Roundtable
https://trumpwhitehouse.archives.gov/briefings-statements/remarks-president-trump-defense-roundtable/

Remarks by President Trump in Roundtable with Hispanic Pastors
https://trumpwhitehouse.archives.gov/briefings-statements/remarks-president-trump-roundtable-hispanic-pastors/

Remarks by President Trump During Roundtable with Hispanic Leaders
https://trumpwhitehouse.archives.gov/briefings-statements/remarks-president-trump-roundtable-hispanic-leaders/

Remarks by President Trump in a Roundtable on Donating Plasma
https://trumpwhitehouse.archives.gov/briefings-statements/remarks-president-trump-roundtable-donating-plasma/

Remarks by President Trump During a Wisconsin Community Safety Roundtable | Kenosha, WI
https://trumpwhitehouse.archives.gov/briefings-statements/remarks-president-trump-wisconsin-community-safety-roundtable-kenosha-wi/

Reason 2. Constitutional Judges

*President Donald J. Trump Is Appointing a Historic Number of
Federal Judges to Uphold Our Constitution as Written*
https://trumpwhitehouse.archives.gov/briefings-
statements/president-donald-j-trump-appointing-historic-
number-federal-judges-uphold-constitution-written/

*Statement from the President on the Passing of Supreme Court
Associate Justice Ruth Bader Ginsburg*
https://trumpwhitehouse.archives.gov/briefings-
statements/statement-president-passing-supreme-court-
associate-justice-ruth-bader-ginsburg/

*WTAS: Support for President Donald J. Trump's Nomination of
Judge Amy Coney Barrett to the Supreme Court*
https://trumpwhitehouse.archives.gov/briefings-
statements/wtas-support-president-donald-j-trumps-
nomination-judge-amy-coney-barrett-supreme-court/

Reason 3. Protecting Free Speech

*President Donald J. Trump is Improving Transparency and
Promoting Free Speech in Higher Education*
https://trumpwhitehouse.archives.gov/briefings-
statements/president-donald-j-trump-is-improving-
transparency-and-promoting-free-speech-in-higher-education/

Preventing Online Censorship
https://www.federalregister.gov/documents/2020/06/02/2020-
12030/preventing-online-censorship

Promoting Free Speech and Religious Liberty
https://www.federalregister.gov/documents/2017/05/09/2017-
09574/promoting-free-speech-and-religious-liberty

Executive Order on Preventing Online Censorship
https://trumpwhitehouse.archives.gov/presidential-
actions/executive-order-preventing-online-censorship/

Reason 4. Religious Rights

*Executive Order on the Establishment of a White House Faith
and Opportunity Initiative*
https://trumpwhitehouse.archives.gov/presidential-
actions/executive-order-establishment-white-house-faith-
opportunity-initiative/

*Remarks by President Trump in Meeting with Inner City
Pastors*
https://trumpwhitehouse.archives.gov/briefings-
statements/remarks-president-trump-meeting-inner-city-
pastors/

Promoting Free Speech and Religious Liberty
https://www.federalregister.gov/documents/2017/05/09/2017-
09574/promoting-free-speech-and-religious-liberty

Reason 5. The Second Amendment

*Remarks by President Trump at the National Rifle Association
Leadership Forum*
https://trumpwhitehouse.archives.gov/briefings-
statements/remarks-president-trump-national-rifle-association-
leadership-forum/

Reason 6. Pro-Life and Protecting the Unborn

*President Donald J. Trump Is Devoted To Protecting American
Freedoms And Promoting American Values*

https://trumpwhitehouse.archives.gov/briefings-
statements/president-donald-j-trump-is-devoted-to-protecting-
american-freedoms-and-promoting-american-values/

Presidential Memorandum Regarding the Mexico City Policy
https://trumpwhitehouse.archives.gov/presidential-
actions/presidential-memorandum-regarding-mexico-city-
policy/

*President Donald J. Trump is Standing Up for the Sanctity of
Life*
https://trumpwhitehouse.archives.gov/briefings-
statements/president-donald-j-trump-standing-sanctity-life/

President Donald J. Trump Signs H.J.Res. 43 into Law
https://trumpwhitehouse.archives.gov/briefings-
statements/president-donald-j-trump-signs-h-j-res-43-law/

*Trump becomes first sitting president to attend March for Life
rally*
https://www.nbcnews.com/politics/donald-trump/trump-
becomes-first-sitting-president-attend-march-life-rally-
n1122246

*Trump Tells Anti-Abortion Marchers, 'Unborn Children Have
Never Had a Stronger Defender in the White House'*
https://www.nytimes.com/2020/01/24/us/politics/trump-
abortion-march-life.html

Statement from the Department of Health and Human Services
https://www.hhs.gov/about/news/2019/06/05/statement-from-
the-department-of-health-and-human-services.html

*United States to Cut Funding to U.N. Population Fund Over
Claims U.N. Calls 'Erroneous'*
https://foreignpolicy.com/2017/04/04/united-states-to-cut-
funding-to-u-n-population-fund-over-claims-u-n-calls-
erroneous/

Funding the United Nations: What Impact Do U.S. Contributions Have on UN Agencies and Programs?
https://www.cfr.org/article/funding-united-nations-what-impact-do-us-contributions-have-un-agencies-and-programs

S.3275 - Pain-Capable Unborn Child Protection Act
https://www.congress.gov/bill/116th-congress/senate-bill/3275

Remarks by President Trump at the 47th Annual March for Life
(Quote)
https://trumpwhitehouse.archives.gov/briefings-statements/remarks-president-trump-47th-annual-march-life/

Executive Order on Protecting Vulnerable Newborn and Infant Children
https://trumpwhitehouse.archives.gov/presidential-actions/executive-order-protecting-vulnerable-newborn-infant-children/

Strengthening the Child Welfare System for America's Children
https://www.federalregister.gov/documents/2020/06/29/2020-14077/strengthening-the-child-welfare-system-for-americas-children

Reason 7. Reining in Regulations

Advancing Responsible Regulatory Reform: The Deregulatory Agenda
https://trumpwhitehouse.archives.gov/articles/advancing-responsible-regulatory-reform-deregulatory-agenda/

Streamlining Permitting and Reducing Regulatory Burdens for Domestic Manufacturing

https://www.federalregister.gov/documents/2017/01/30/2017-
02044/streamlining-permitting-and-reducing-regulatory-
burdens-for-domestic-manufacturing

*Executive Order 13789-Second Report to the President on
Identifying and Reducing Tax Regulatory Burdens*
https://www.federalregister.gov/documents/2017/10/16/2017-
22205/executive-order-13789-second-report-to-the-president-
on-identifying-and-reducing-tax-regulatory

*H.R.1177 - Removing Outdated Restrictions to Allow for Job
Growth Act*
https://www.congress.gov/bill/115th-congress/house-bill/1177

Reason 8. Building the Wall

Border Wall System video
https://www.cbp.gov/border-security/along-us-borders/border-
wall-system

*Remarks by President Trump During Border Wall
Construction and Operational Update | Yuma, AZ*
https://trumpwhitehouse.archives.gov/briefings-
statements/remarks-president-trump-border-wall-construction-
operational-update-yuma-az/

Reason 9. The COVID-19 Shutdown Decision

Remarks by President Trump on Actions Against China
https://trumpwhitehouse.archives.gov/briefings-
statements/remarks-president-trump-actions-china/

*Remarks by President Trump and Vice President Pence in
Roundtable with Industry Executives on the Plan for Opening
Up America Again*

https://trumpwhitehouse.archives.gov/briefings-
statements/remarks-president-trump-vice-president-pence-
roundtable-industry-executives-plan-opening-america/

Reason 10. Removing the Obamacare Mandate

*Minimizing the Economic Burden of the Patient Protection and
Affordable Care Act Pending Repeal*
https://www.federalregister.gov/documents/2017/01/24/2017-
01799/minimizing-the-economic-burden-of-the-patient-
protection-and-affordable-care-act-pending-repeal

*Remarks by President Trump on the America First Healthcare
Plan*
https://trumpwhitehouse.archives.gov/briefings-
statements/remarks-president-trump-america-first-healthcare-
plan/

Reason 11. President Trump Signs GOP Tax Reform Bill

*H.R.1 - An Act to provide for reconciliation pursuant to titles II
and V of the concurrent resolution on the budget for fiscal year
2018*
https://www.congress.gov/bill/115th-congress/house-bill/1

H. R. 1
https://www.congress.gov/115/bills/hr1/BILLS-115hr1enr.pdf

Tax cuts hit home
https://trumpwhitehouse.archives.gov/briefings-
statements/washington-times-tax-cuts-hit-home/

*Tax Cuts and Reforms are Helping American Workers and
Businesses*
https://trumpwhitehouse.archives.gov/briefings-statements/tax-
cuts-reforms-helping-american-workers-businesses/

Trump signs sweeping tax bill into law
https://www.washingtonpost.com/news/post-
politics/wp/2017/12/22/trump-signs-sweeping-tax-bill-into-
law/

2017 1st Quarter Manufacturers' Outlook Survey
https://www.nam.org/2017-1st-quarter-manufacturers-outlook-
survey/

Reason 12. U.S. Energy Independence

*Executive Order 13795—Implementing an America-First
Offshore Energy Strategy*
https://www.presidency.ucsb.edu/documents/executive-order-
13795-implementing-america-first-offshore-energy-strategy

*DCPD-201700287 - Executive Order 13795-Implementing an
America-First Offshore Energy Strategy*
https://www.govinfo.gov/app/details/DCPD-201700287

The Value of U.S. Energy Dominance
https://trumpwhitehouse.archives.gov/articles/value-u-s-
energy-dominance/

Executive Order 13795; EO 13795
https://www.hsdl.org/?abstract&did=800693

*The United States Was Energy Independent in 2019 for the
First Time Since 1957*
https://www.instituteforenergyresearch.org/fossil-fuels/gas-
and-oil/the-united-states-was-energy-independent-in-2019-for-
the-first-time-since-1957/

Reason 13. USMCA Trade

States sources
USMCA State Fact Sheets
https://ustr.gov/about-us/policy-offices/press-office/fact-sheets/2018/october/usmca-state-fact-sheets

Trade sources
Agreement between the United States of America, the United Mexican States, and Canada 12/13/19 Text
https://ustr.gov/trade-agreements/free-trade-agreements/united-states-mexico-canada-agreement/agreement-between

Joe Biden says Trump's USMCA is 'better than NAFTA'
https://nypost.com/2020/09/11/joe-biden-admits-trumps-usmca-is-better-than-nafta/

WTAS: Support for President Donald J. Trump's United States-Mexico-Canada Agreement
https://trumpwhitehouse.archives.gov/briefings-statements/wtas-support-president-donald-j-trumps-united-states-mexico-canada-agreement/

President Donald J. Trump Secured a Better Deal for America with USMCA
https://trumpwhitehouse.archives.gov/briefings-statements/president-donald-j-trump-secured-better-deal-america-usmca/

Remarks by Vice President Pence at Auto Industry Discussion of the United States-Mexico-Canada Agreement Taylor, Michigan
https://trumpwhitehouse.archives.gov/briefings-statements/remarks-vice-president-pence-auto-industry-discussion-united-states-mexico-canada-agreement-taylor-michigan/

President Donald J. Trump Has Forged New Trade Agreements to Revitalize American Industry and Agriculture
https://trumpwhitehouse.archives.gov/briefings-statements/president-donald-j-trump-forged-new-trade-agreements-revitalize-american-industry/

Reason 14. Support for Veterans and VA

Enough is enough: Trump gave veterans real and permanent choice
https://thehill.com/blogs/congress-blog/healthcare/513958-enough-is-enough-trump-gave-veterans-real-and-permanent-choice

Remarks by President Trump and Veterans Affairs Secretary Shulkin at Veterans Affairs Listening Session
https://trumpwhitehouse.archives.gov/briefings-statements/remarks-president-trump-veterans-affairs-secretary-shulkin-veterans-affairs-listening-session/

White House Listening Session on Veterans Affairs
https://www.c-span.org/video/?425590-1/president-trump-plan-reform-va-ahead-schedule

Presidential Memorandum on Discharging the Federal Student Loan Debt of Totally and Permanently Disabled Veterans
https://trumpwhitehouse.archives.gov/presidential-actions/presidential-memorandum-discharging-federal-student-loan-debt-totally-permanently-disabled-veterans/

Reason 15. The 1776 Project

Patriotic History Is Comparative History
https://www.nationalreview.com/2020/09/1776-commission-patriotic-history-comparative-history/#slide-1

President Trump is Fighting Harmful Ideologies that Cause Division in Our Federal Workplaces
https://trumpwhitehouse.archives.gov/briefings-statements/president-trump-fighting-harmful-ideologies-cause-division-federal-workplaces/

Remarks by President Trump at the White House Conference on American History
https://trumpwhitehouse.archives.gov/briefings-statements/remarks-president-trump-white-house-conference-american-history/

Remarks by President Trump at the 2020 Salute to America
https://trumpwhitehouse.archives.gov/briefings-statements/remarks-president-trump-2020-salute-america/

Remarks by President Trump at South Dakota's 2020 Mount Rushmore Fireworks Celebration | Keystone, South Dakota
https://trumpwhitehouse.archives.gov/briefings-statements/remarks-president-trump-south-dakotas-2020-mount-rushmore-fireworks-celebration-keystone-south-dakota/

Presidential Message on the 244th Anniversary of the Adoption of the Declaration of Independence
https://trumpwhitehouse.archives.gov/briefings-statements/presidential-message-244th-anniversary-adoption-declaration-independence/

Reason 16. Standing Up to Socialism

Remarks by President Trump in State of the Union Address
https://trumpwhitehouse.archives.gov/briefings-statements/remarks-president-trump-state-union-address-3/

Remarks by President Trump in State of the Union Address
https://trumpwhitehouse.archives.gov/briefings-statements/remarks-president-trump-state-union-address-2/

Proclamation 9873 of April 30, 2019
https://www.govinfo.gov/content/pkg/FR-2019-05-06/html/2019-09327.htm

H. Res. 253 (IH) - Recognizing that it is the sense of the United States House of Representatives that Socialism poses a significant threat to the freedom, liberty, and economic prosperity.
https://www.govinfo.gov/app/details/BILLS-116hres253ih

165 Cong. Rec. S5148 - SENATE RESOLUTION 289--EXPRESSING THE SENSE OF THE SENATE THAT SOCIALISM POSES A SIGNIFICANT THREAT TO FREEDOM, LIBERTY, AND ECONOMIC PROSPERITY
https://www.govinfo.gov/app/details/CREC-2019-07-29/CREC-2019-07-29-pt1-PgS5148

S. Res. 289 (IS) - Expressing the sense of the Senate that socialism poses a significant threat to freedom, liberty, and economic prosperity.
https://www.govinfo.gov/app/details/BILLS-116sres289is

84 FR 19695 - Loyalty Day, 2019
https://www.govinfo.gov/app/details/FR-2019-05-06/2019-09327

Reason 17. Calm in the Face of the Coronavirus Storm

Remarks by President Trump at Naval Station Norfolk Send-Off for USNS Comfort | Norfolk, VA
https://trumpwhitehouse.archives.gov/briefings-statements/remarks-president-trump-naval-station-norfolk-send-off-usns-comfort-norfolk-va/

Remarks by President Trump in a Meeting with Supply Chain Distributors on COVID-19
https://trumpwhitehouse.archives.gov/briefings-statements/remarks-president-trump-meeting-supply-chain-distributors-COVID-19/

Remarks by President Trump on the Farmers to Families Food Box Program Distribution | Mills River, NC
https://trumpwhitehouse.archives.gov/briefings-statements/remarks-president-trump-farmers-families-food-box-program-distribution-mills-river-nc/

Several Michigan Companies Awarded Contracts for USDA Farm to Families Food Box Program
https://www.michigan.gov/coronavirus/0,9753,7-406-98158-528880--,00.html

USDA Announces a Third Round of Farmers to Families Food Box Program Purchases
https://www.usda.gov/media/press-releases/2020/07/24/usda-announces-third-round-farmers-families-food-box-program

USDA to Purchase Up to $3 Billion in Agricultural Commodities, Issue Solicitations for Interested Participants
https://www.ams.usda.gov/content/usda-purchase-3-billion-agricultural-commodities-issue-solicitations-interested

H.R.6201 - Families First Coronavirus Response Act
https://www.congress.gov/bill/116th-congress/house-bill/6201

President Donald J. Trump Is Protecting America's Food Supply Chain and Ensuring No Family Goes Hungry
https://trumpwhitehouse.archives.gov/briefings-statements/president-donald-j-trump-protecting-americas-food-supply-chain-ensuring-no-family-goes-hungry/

White House announces $750M deal for Abbott Labs' COVID-19 rapid test
https://www.foxbusiness.com/healthcare/white-house-to-give-abbott-labs-750m-for-covid-19-rapid-test

President Donald J. Trump and His Administration Have Created The Best Covid-19 Testing System In The World
https://trumpwhitehouse.archives.gov/briefings-statements/president-donald-j-trump-administration-created-best-COVID-19-testing-system-world/

Remarks by Vice President Pence in a Roundtable on Phase 3 COVID-19 Vaccine Trials | Miami, FL
https://trumpwhitehouse.archives.gov/briefings-statements/remarks-vice-president-pence-roundtable-phase-3-COVID-19-vaccine-trials-miami-fl/

Remarks by President Trump in a Meeting with Supply Chain Distributors on COVID-19
https://trumpwhitehouse.archives.gov/briefings-statements/remarks-president-trump-meeting-supply-chain-distributors-COVID-19/

President Donald J. Trump and His Administration Have Created The Best Covid-19 Testing System In The World
https://trumpwhitehouse.archives.gov/briefings-statements/president-donald-j-trump-administration-created-best-COVID-19-testing-system-world/

HUD PROVIDES IMMEDIATE RELIEF FOR HOMEOWNERS AMID NATIONWIDE CORONAVIRUS RESPONSE
https://www.hud.gov/press/press_releases_media_advisories/HUD_No_20_042

H.R.748 - CARES Act
https://www.congress.gov/bill/116th-congress/house-bill/748

Executive Order on Fighting the Spread of COVID-19 by Providing Assistance to Renters and Homeowners
https://trumpwhitehouse.archives.gov/presidential-actions/executive-order-fighting-spread-COVID-19-providing-assistance-renters-homeowners/

Memorandum on Continued Student Loan Payment Relief During the COVID-19 Pandemic
https://trumpwhitehouse.archives.gov/presidential-actions/memorandum-continued-student-loan-payment-relief-COVID-19-pandemic/

Memorandum on Deferring Payroll Tax Obligations in Light of the Ongoing COVID-19 Disaster
https://trumpwhitehouse.archives.gov/presidential-actions/memorandum-deferring-payroll-tax-obligations-light-ongoing-COVID-19-disaster/

Remarks by President Trump at Signing of the Coronavirus Preparedness and Response Supplemental Appropriations Act, 2020
https://trumpwhitehouse.archives.gov/briefings-statements/remarks-president-trump-signing-coronavirus-preparedness-response-supplemental-appropriations-act-2020/

President Donald J. Trump Is Committed to Supporting Small Businesses Impacted by the Coronavirus
https://trumpwhitehouse.archives.gov/briefings-statements/president-donald-j-trump-committed-supporting-small-businesses-impacted-coronavirus/

Reason 18. Retooling Manufacturing for COVID-19 Emergency

10 Companies Retool to Support Health Care Workers: COVID-19 Crisis https://www.patientcareonline.com/view/10-companies-retool-support-health-care-workers-covid-19-crisis

Remarks by President Trump at Honeywell International Inc. Mask Production Facility | Phoenix, AZ
https://trumpwhitehouse.archives.gov/briefings-statements/remarks-president-trump-honeywell-international-inc-mask-production-facility-phoenix-az/

Statement from the President Regarding the Defense Production Act
https://trumpwhitehouse.archives.gov/briefings-statements/statement-president-regarding-defense-production-act/

Statement from the President Regarding the Defense Production Act
https://trumpwhitehouse.archives.gov/briefings-statements/statement-president-regarding-defense-production-act-2/

COALITION OF ICONIC AMERICAN APPAREL BRANDS & TEXTILE COMPANIES HEEDS CALL OF NATION TO PRODUCE MEDICAL FACE MASKS
http://www.ncto.org/coalition-of-iconic-american-apparel-brands-textile-companies-heeds-call-of-nation-to-produce-medical-face-masks/

15 Companies Retooling Their Operations to Fight COVID-19
https://www.triplepundit.com/story/2020/companies-retooling-operations-COVID-19/88921

MyPillow shifting 75% of production to make face masks for hospitals
https://www.fox29.com/news/mypillow-shifting-75-of-production-to-make-face-masks-for-hospitals

Reason 19. Operation Warp Speed to a COVID-19 Vaccine

President Donald J. Trump Is Promoting Safe Plasma Donations To Protect Americans And Defeat COVID-19
https://trumpwhitehouse.archives.gov/briefings-statements/president-donald-j-trump-promoting-safe-plasma-donations-protect-americans-defeat-COVID-19/

President Donald J. Trump Is Using Every Available Resource to Deliver a Safe and Effective Vaccine to the American People
https://trumpwhitehouse.archives.gov/briefings-statements/president-donald-j-trump-using-every-available-resource-deliver-safe-effective-vaccine-american-people/

President Donald J. Trump is Ensuring that Essential Medical Supplies are Produced in the United States
https://trumpwhitehouse.archives.gov/briefings-statements/president-donald-j-trump-ensuring-essential-medical-supplies-produced-united-states/

Johnson & Johnson launches massive human trial of COVID-19 vaccine
https://www.washingtontimes.com/news/2020/sep/23/johnson-johnson-launches-massive-human-trial-covid/

President Donald J. Trump Is Using Every Available Resource to Deliver a Safe and Effective Vaccine to the American People
https://trumpwhitehouse.archives.gov/briefings-statements/president-donald-j-trump-using-every-available-resource-deliver-safe-effective-vaccine-american-people/

Reason 20. Law & Order

Trump Administration Keeps its Promise: Begins Removing Violent Gang Members, Criminals, and Predators from American Communities

https://trumpwhitehouse.archives.gov/briefings-
statements/trump-administration-keeps-promise-begins-
removing-violent-gang-members-criminals-predators-
american-communities/

*After Two Deaths During Kenosha Protests, Trump Sending
Federal Troops to 'Restore Law and Order'*
https://www.newsweek.com/after-2-deaths-during-kenosha-
protests-trump-sending-federal-troops-restore-law-order-
1527849

*H.R. 2379 / Public Law No. 116–18 To reauthorize the
Bulletproof Vest Partnership Grant Program.*
https://www.congress.gov/bill/116th-congress/house-bill/2379

*Remarks by President Trump on Operation LeGend:
Combatting Violent Crime in American Cities*
https://trumpwhitehouse.archives.gov/briefings-
statements/remarks-president-trump-operation-legend-
combatting-violent-crime-american-cities/

*Memorandum on Reviewing Funding to State and Local
Government Recipients That Are Permitting Anarchy,
Violence, and Destruction in American Cities*
https://trumpwhitehouse.archives.gov/presidential-
actions/memorandum-reviewing-funding-state-local-
government-recipients-permitting-anarchy-violence-
destruction-american-cities/

*Executive Order on Protecting American Monuments,
Memorials, and Statues and Combating Recent Criminal
Violence*
https://trumpwhitehouse.archives.gov/presidential-
actions/executive-order-protecting-american-monuments-
memorials-statues-combating-recent-criminal-violence/

Reason 21. U.S. Pipelines

Presidential Memorandum Regarding Construction of American Pipelines
https://trumpwhitehouse.archives.gov/presidential-actions/presidential-memorandum-regarding-construction-american-pipelines/

Presidential Memorandum Regarding Construction of the Keystone XL Pipeline
https://trumpwhitehouse.archives.gov/presidential-actions/presidential-memorandum-regarding-construction-keystone-xl-pipeline/

President Trump Takes Action to Expedite Priority Energy and Infrastructure Projects
https://trumpwhitehouse.archives.gov/briefings-statements/president-trump-takes-action-expedite-priority-energy-infrastructure-projects/

Presidential Memorandum Regarding Construction of American Pipelines
https://trumpwhitehouse.archives.gov/the-press-office/2017/01/24/presidential-memorandum-regarding-construction-american-pipelines

Presidential Permit
https://trumpwhitehouse.archives.gov/presidential-actions/presidential-permit-072920-3/

Presidential Permit
https://trumpwhitehouse.archives.gov/presidential-actions/presidential-permit-072920/

Presidential Permit
https://trumpwhitehouse.archives.gov/presidential-actions/presidential-permit-072920-4/

Reason 22. Supporting Historically Black Colleges and Universities

Trump signs bill restoring funding for black colleges
https://apnews.com/c4834e48841d97c5a93312b1bf75302a

Readout of the White House Historically Black Colleges & Universities (HBCUs) Leadership Listening Session
https://trumpwhitehouse.archives.gov/briefings-statements/readout-white-house-historically-black-colleges-universities-hbcus-leadership-listening-session/

Federal TRIO Programs
https://www2.ed.gov/about/offices/list/ope/trio/index.html

Reason 23. Jobs, Jobs, Jobs

Remarks by President Trump in Listening Session with the Retail Industry Leaders Association and Member Company CEOs
https://trumpwhitehouse.archives.gov/briefings-statements/remarks-president-trump-listening-session-retail-industry-leaders-association-member-company-ceos/

Reinvesting in the American Workforce
https://trumpwhitehouse.archives.gov/articles/reinvesting-american-workforce/

Nurturing a Small Business Boon
https://trumpwhitehouse.archives.gov/articles/nurturing-small-business-boon/

Pro-Growth, Pro-Jobs, Pro-Worker, Pro-Family, and Pro-America
https://trumpwhitehouse.archives.gov/articles/pro-growth-pro-jobs-pro-worker-pro-family-pro-america/

Reason 24. Apprenticeships & Vocational Education

Trump Administration's Industry-Recognized Apprenticeships Will Keep America Working
https://trumpwhitehouse.archives.gov/articles/trump-administrations-industry-recognized-apprenticeships-will-keep-america-working/

Remarks by President Trump at Parent-Teacher Conference Listening Session
https://trumpwhitehouse.archives.gov/briefings-statements/remarks-president-trump-parent-teacher-conference-listening-session/

Remarks by President Trump in Parent-Teacher Conference Listening Session
https://trumpwhitehouse.archives.gov/briefings-statements/remarks-president-trump-parent-teacher-conference-listening-session-2/

Remarks by President Trump at Signing of an Executive Order on Apprenticeship and Workforce of Tomorrow Initiatives
(Quote)
https://trumpwhitehouse.archives.gov/briefings-statements/remarks-president-trump-signing-executive-order-apprenticeship-workforce-tomorrow-initiatives/

Trump Administration's Industry-Recognized Apprenticeships Will Keep America Working
https://trumpwhitehouse.archives.gov/articles/trump-administrations-industry-recognized-apprenticeships-will-keep-america-working/

Statement from the President on the Passage of Legislation to Reauthorize the Carl D. Perkins Career and Technical Education Act
https://trumpwhitehouse.archives.gov/briefings-statements/statement-president-passage-legislation-reauthorize-carl-d-perkins-career-technical-education-act/

H.R.2353 - Strengthening Career and Technical Education for the 21st Century Act
https://www.congress.gov/bill/115th-congress/house-bill/2353

The Perkins Act Has Finally Been Reauthorized. Here's What's In It and Why It Matters to MN
https://www.educationevolving.org/blog/2018/08/perkins-act-reauthorized

WHAT WAS THE PRESIDENTIAL EXECUTIVE ORDER ABOUT APPRENTICESHIPS AND WHERE CAN I FIND MORE INFORMATION?
https://www.apprenticeship.gov/help/what-was-presidential-executive-order-about-apprenticeships-and-where-can-i-find-more

TASK FORCE ON APPRENTICESHIP EXPANSION: Final Report to: The President of the United States
https://www.dol.gov/apprenticeship/docs/task-force-apprenticeship-expansion-report.pdf

Reason 25. Defense & Military Build Up

Remarks by President Trump at Signing of H.R. 2810, National Defense Authorization Act for FY2018
https://trumpwhitehouse.archives.gov/briefings-statements/remarks-president-trump-signing-h-r-2810-national-defense-authorization-act-fy2018/

152

President Donald J. Trump Is Fulfilling His Promise to Rebuild Our Nation's Military and Support Our Troops
https://trumpwhitehouse.archives.gov/briefings-statements/president-donald-j-trump-fulfilling-promise-rebuild-nations-military-support-troops/

Defense
https://www.heritage.org/defense

Remarks by President Trump in Press Briefing
https://trumpwhitehouse.archives.gov/briefings-statements/remarks-president-trump-press-briefing-091020/

Reason 26. Getting the U.S. out of NAFTA

President Donald J. Trump is Keeping His Promise to Renegotiate NAFTA
https://trumpwhitehouse.archives.gov/briefings-statements/president-donald-j-trump-keeping-promise-renegotiate-nafta/

Statement from the Press Secretary Regarding Senate Passage of the USMCA
https://trumpwhitehouse.archives.gov/briefings-statements/statement-press-secretary-regarding-senate-passage-usmca/

Trump's NAFTA Changes
https://www.thebalance.com/donald-trump-nafta-4111368

U.S. – Mexico – Canada Agreement (USMCA)
https://www.cbp.gov/trade/priority-issues/trade-agreements/free-trade-agreements/USMCA

Agreement between the United States of America, the United Mexican States, and Canada 12/13/19 Text https://ustr.gov/trade-agreements/free-trade-agreements/united-states-mexico-canada-agreement/agreement-between

United States-Mexico-Canada Agreement
https://ustr.gov/trade-agreements/free-trade-agreements/united-states-mexico-canada-agreement

FINAL VOTE RESULTS FOR ROLL CALL 701
http://clerk.house.gov/evs/2019/roll701.xml

Reason 27. Record Breaking Employment

The Employment Situation - January 2017
https://www.bls.gov/news.release/archives/empsit_02032017.pdf

Unemployment rates in Arkansas and Oregon at record lows in February 2017
https://www.bls.gov/opub/ted/2017/unemployment-rates-in-arkansas-and-oregon-at-record-lows-in-february-2017.htm

The Economics Daily
https://www.bls.gov/opub/ted/metropolitan-areas-and-counties.htm

The Economics Daily
https://blogs.wsj.com/economics/2017/08/08/u-s-job-openings-climb-to-record-6-2-million-at-end-of-june/

Overview of BLS Statistics on Unemployment
https://www.bls.gov/bls/unemployment.htm

Civilian unemployment rate
https://www.bls.gov/charts/employment-situation/civilian-unemployment-rate.htm

Under President Donald J. Trump, Americans Are Getting Back To Work
https://trumpwhitehouse.archives.gov/briefings-statements/president-donald-j-trump-americans-getting-back-work/

The Historic Results Of President Donald J. Trump's Economic Agenda
https://trumpwhitehouse.archives.gov/briefings-statements/historic-results-president-donald-j-trumps-economic-agenda/

America's Unemployment Rate Falls to Its Lowest Level in Almost 50 Years
https://trumpwhitehouse.archives.gov/articles/americas-unemployment-rate-falls-lowest-level-almost-50-years/

Reason 28. Bringing Back Mining

Why President Trump Overhauled Obama's Coal Emissions Standards
https://www.heritage.org/coal-oil-natural-gas/heritage-explains/why-president-trump-overhauled-obamas-coal-emissions

May 2019 National Industry-Specific Occupational Employment and Wage Estimates
https://www.bls.gov/oes/current/naics4_212100.htm

Coal mine starts continue to decline
https://www.eia.gov/todayinenergy/detail.php?id=23052

Flashback 2008: Obama Promised To 'Bankrupt' Coal Companies
https://dailycaller.com/2015/08/03/flashback-2008-obama-promised-to-bankrupt-coal-companies/

Obama Kept His Promise, 83,000 Coal Jobs Lost And 400 Mines Shuttered
https://dailycaller.com/2016/09/05/obama-kept-his-promise-83000-coal-jobs-lost-and-400-mines-shuttered/

Carbon Pollution Emission Guidelines for Existing Stationary Sources: Electric Utility Generating Units
https://www.federalregister.gov/documents/2015/10/23/2015-22842/carbon-pollution-emission-guidelines-for-existing-stationary-sources-electric-utility-generating

Review of the Clean Power Plan
https://www.federalregister.gov/documents/2017/04/04/2017-06522/review-of-the-clean-power-plan

Repeal of the Clean Power Plan; Emission Guidelines for Greenhouse Gas Emissions From Existing Electric Utility Generating Units; Revisions to Emission Guidelines Implementing Regulations
https://www.federalregister.gov/documents/2019/07/08/2019-13507/repeal-of-the-clean-power-plan-emission-guidelines-for-greenhouse-gas-emissions-from-existing

WTAS: Support for the Trump Administration's Proposal to Replace the Costly and Overreaching Clean Power Plan
https://trumpwhitehouse.archives.gov/briefings-statements/wtas-support-trump-administrations-proposal-replace-costly-overreaching-clean-power-plan/

The Value of U.S. Energy Dominance
https://trumpwhitehouse.archives.gov/articles/value-u-s-energy-dominance/

Reason 29. U.S. Embassy Moves to Jerusalem

DCPD-201700887 - Proclamation 9683-Recognizing Jerusalem as the Capital of the State of Israel and Relocating the United States Embassy to Israel to Jerusalem
https://www.govinfo.gov/app/details/DCPD-201700887

JERUSALEM EMBASSY ACT OF 1995
https://www.congress.gov/104/plaws/publ45/PLAW-104publ45.pdf

Reason 30. ISIS Defeated

Remarks by President Trump on the Killing of Qasem Soleimani
https://trumpwhitehouse.archives.gov/briefings-statements/remarks-president-trump-killing-qasem-soleimani/

Remarks by President Trump on the Death of ISIS Leader Abu Bakr al-Baghdadi
https://trumpwhitehouse.archives.gov/briefings-statements/remarks-president-trump-death-isis-leader-abu-bakr-al-baghdadi/

Presidential Memorandum Plan to Defeat the Islamic State of Iraq and Syria
https://trumpwhitehouse.archives.gov/presidential-actions/presidential-memorandum-plan-defeat-islamic-state-iraq-syria/

Reason 31. Prescription Drug Reform

Executive Order on Lowering Drug Prices by Putting America First
https://trumpwhitehouse.archives.gov/presidential-
actions/executive-order-lowering-drug-prices-putting-america-
first/

Lowering Prices for Patients by Eliminating Kickbacks to Middlemen
https://www.federalregister.gov/documents/2020/07/29/2020-
16625/lowering-prices-for-patients-by-eliminating-kickbacks-
to-middlemen

Executive Order on An America-First Healthcare Plan
https://trumpwhitehouse.archives.gov/presidential-
actions/executive-order-america-first-healthcare-plan/

Reason 32. The Opioid Crisis

Remarks by President Trump in Listening Session on Opioids and Drug Abuse
https://trumpwhitehouse.archives.gov/briefings-
statements/remarks-president-trump-listening-session-opioids-
drug-abuse/

On-The-Record Press Call on the Youth Opioid Prevention Ad Campaign
https://trumpwhitehouse.archives.gov/briefings-
statements/record-press-call-youth-opioid-prevention-ad-
campaign/

Reason 33. The Right to Try

S.204 - Trickett Wendler, Frank Mongiello, Jordan McLinn, and Matthew Bellina Right to Try Act of 2017
https://www.congress.gov/bill/115th-congress/senate-bill/204

Reason 34. Healthcare and Preexisting Conditions

Remarks by President Trump in Listening Session with Health Insurance Company CEOs
https://trumpwhitehouse.archives.gov/briefings-statements/remarks-president-trump-listening-session-health-insurance-company-ceos/

Remarks by President Trump at Signing of H.R. 3401
https://trumpwhitehouse.archives.gov/briefings-statements/remarks-president-trump-signing-h-r-3401/

Remarks by President Trump at a Fox News Town Hall, Scranton, PA
https://trumpwhitehouse.archives.gov/briefings-statements/remarks-president-trump-fox-news-town-hall-scranton-pa/

Remarks by President Trump at Signing of Executive Order on Advancing American Kidney Health
https://trumpwhitehouse.archives.gov/briefings-statements/remarks-president-trump-signing-executive-order-advancing-american-kidney-health/

Remarks by President Trump at the White House Business Session with our Nation's Governors
https://trumpwhitehouse.archives.gov/briefings-statements/remarks-president-trump-white-house-business-session-nations-governors/

Remarks by President Trump on Expanding Health Coverage Options for Small Businesses and Workers
https://trumpwhitehouse.archives.gov/briefings-statements/remarks-president-trump-expanding-health-coverage-options-small-businesses-workers/

President Trump Is Working To Ensure That Every American Has Access To Better Healthcare At Lower Cost
https://trumpwhitehouse.archives.gov/briefings-statements/president-trump-working-ensure-every-american-access-better-healthcare-lower-cost/

President Donald J. Trump Is Taking Action to Lower Drug Costs and Ensure That Americans Have Access to Life-saving Medications
https://trumpwhitehouse.archives.gov/briefings-statements/president-donald-j-trump-taking-action-lower-drug-costs-ensure-americans-access-life-saving-medications/

Access to Affordable Life-Saving Medications
https://www.federalregister.gov/documents/2020/07/29/2020-16623/access-to-affordable-life-saving-medications

Implementation of Executive Order 13937, "Executive Order on Access to Affordable Life-Saving Medications"
https://www.federalregister.gov/documents/2020/09/28/2020-21358/implementation-of-executive-order-13937-executive-order-on-access-to-affordable-life-saving

Executive Order on An America-First Healthcare Plan
https://trumpwhitehouse.archives.gov/presidential-actions/executive-order-america-first-healthcare-plan/

Reason 35. Border Control & Immigration

Proclamation on Amendment to Proclamation 10052
https://trumpwhitehouse.archives.gov/presidential-
actions/proclamation-amendment-proclamation-10052/

*Remarks by President Trump in Roundtable on Border
Security, Yuma, AZ*
https://trumpwhitehouse.archives.gov/briefings-
statements/remarks-president-trump-roundtable-border-
security-yuma-az/

*President Donald J. Trump Is Taking Action to Ensure
American Citizens Receive Proper Representation in Congress*
https://trumpwhitehouse.archives.gov/briefings-
statements/president-donald-j-trump-taking-action-ensure-
american-citizens-receive-proper-representation-congress/

*Remarks by President Trump During Border Wall
Construction and Operational Update, Yuma, AZ*
https://trumpwhitehouse.archives.gov/briefings-
statements/remarks-president-trump-border-wall-construction-
operational-update-yuma-az/

*Abolishing ICE Would Erase America's Borders And Open The
Floodgates To More Crime, Drugs, And Terrorism*
https://trumpwhitehouse.archives.gov/briefings-
statements/abolishing-ice-erase-americas-borders-open-
floodgates-crime-drugs-terrorism/

Statement from the Press Secretary
https://trumpwhitehouse.archives.gov/briefings-
statements/statement-press-secretary-108/

*U.S. Asylum Pact With Honduras Cements Trump
Administration's Regional Strategy*
https://www.wsj.com/articles/trump-administration-uses-u-s-
leverage-to-seal-migration-deals-11569415931

Fact Sheet: DHS Agreements with Guatemala, Honduras, and El Salvador
https://www.dhs.gov/sites/default/files/publications/19_1028_o
pa_factsheet-northern-central-america-agreements_v2.pdf

Remarks by President Trump at Signing of Safe Third Country Agreement with Guatemala
https://trumpwhitehouse.archives.gov/briefings-
statements/remarks-president-trump-signing-safe-third-
country-agreement-guatemala/

8 U.S. Code § 1158 - Asylum
https://www.law.cornell.edu/uscode/text/8/1158

8 U.S.C. 1158 - Asylum
https://www.govinfo.gov/app/details/USCODE-2015-
title8/USCODE-2015-title8-chap12-subchapII-partI-sec1158

Proclamation on Addressing Mass Migration Through the Southern Border of the United States
https://trumpwhitehouse.archives.gov/presidential-
actions/proclamation-addressing-mass-migration-southern-
border-united-states/

A Look at Mexican Efforts to Stem Tide of Migrants
https://www.voanews.com/usa/us-politics/look-mexican-
efforts-stem-tide-migrants

What the Safe Third Country Deals Mean for The Future of Asylum in the United States
https://immigrationimpact.com/2019/10/04/safe-third-country-
deals-asylum/#.X2Y86sHYq1s

Mexico Begins Detaining Central American Migrants in Caravans
https://www.wsj.com/articles/mexico-cracks-down-on-
caravans-of-central-american-migrants-11556047683

US, Mexico seek to stem migration from Central America by funding development in region
https://www.usatoday.com/story/news/world/2018/12/18/u-s-mexico-cooperate-plans-reduce-central-american-migration/2355627002/

Proclamation on Amendment to Proclamation 10052
https://trumpwhitehouse.archives.gov/presidential-actions/proclamation-amendment-proclamation-10052/

President Donald J. Trump Is Taking Action to Ensure American Citizens Receive Proper Representation in Congress
https://trumpwhitehouse.archives.gov/briefings-statements/president-donald-j-trump-taking-action-ensure-american-citizens-receive-proper-representation-congress/

Statement from the Press Secretary
https://trumpwhitehouse.archives.gov/briefings-statements/statement-press-secretary-091220/

Affording Congress an Opportunity To Address Family Separation
https://www.federalregister.gov/documents/2018/06/25/2018-13696/affording-congress-an-opportunity-to-address-family-separation

Executive Order: Border Security and Immigration Enforcement Improvements
https://trumpwhitehouse.archives.gov/presidential-actions/executive-order-border-security-immigration-enforcement-improvements/

Report on Ending "Catch and Release" at the Borders of the United States
https://www.aila.org/File/Related/19092405a.pdf

Federal policy on border security, 2017-2020
https://ballotpedia.org/Federal_policy_on_border_security,_20
17-2020

SBInet Independent Assessment: Analysis of Alternatives, Phase IA
https://foiarr.cbp.gov/docs/Border_Wall_Records/2018/102111
4406_2129/1805310839_BW_FOIA_CBP_000498___000597.
pdf

The History of the Flores Settlement
https://cis.org/Report/History-Flores-Settlement

Reason 36. U.S. Medicine Security

Trump takes a first step toward returning medical supply chains to the U.S.
https://www.washingtonpost.com/business/2020/05/19/trump-
takes-first-step-toward-returning-medical-supply-chains-us/

Bringing drug production back to the US
https://cen.acs.org/business/outsourcing/Bringing-drug-
production-back-US/98/i25

Remarks by President Trump, Vice President Pence, and Members of the Coronavirus Task Force in Press Briefing
https://trumpwhitehouse.archives.gov/briefings-
statements/remarks-president-trump-vice-president-pence-
members-coronavirus-task-force-press-briefing-21/

Momentum grows to change medical supply chain from China
https://thehill.com/policy/national-security/491119-
momentum-grows-to-change-medical-supply-chain-from-china

Rubio, Colleagues Introduce the Strengthening America's Supply Chain and National Security Act
https://www.rubio.senate.gov/public/index.cfm/2020/3/rubio-colleagues-introduce-the-strengthening-america-s-supply-chain-and-national-security-act

Trump Order to Buy U.S.-Made Medical Supplies Coming Soon: Navarro
https://www.usnews.com/news/us/articles/2020-05-04/trump-orders-to-address-medical-supplies-energy-components-navarro

Remarks by President Trump in Roundtable Discussion with Industry Executives on Reopening
https://trumpwhitehouse.archives.gov/briefings-statements/remarks-president-trump-roundtable-discussion-industry-executives-reopening/

Executive Order on Ensuring Essential Medicines, Medical Countermeasures, and Critical Inputs Are Made in the United States
https://trumpwhitehouse.archives.gov/presidential-actions/executive-order-ensuring-essential-medicines-medical-countermeasures-critical-inputs-made-united-states/

President Donald J. Trump is Ensuring that Essential Medical Supplies are Produced in the United States
https://trumpwhitehouse.archives.gov/briefings-statements/president-donald-j-trump-ensuring-essential-medical-supplies-produced-united-states/

Reason 37. U.S. Food and Water Security

Presidential Executive Order on Assessing and Strengthening the Manufacturing and Defense Industrial Base and Supply Chain Resiliency of the United States

https://trumpwhitehouse.archives.gov/presidential-
actions/presidential-executive-order-assessing-strengthening-
manufacturing-defense-industrial-base-supply-chain-resiliency-
united-states/

*Executive Order on Delegating Authority Under the DPA with
Respect to Food Supply Chain Resources During the National
Emergency Caused by the Outbreak of COVID-19*
https://trumpwhitehouse.archives.gov/presidential-
actions/executive-order-delegating-authority-dpa-respect-food-
supply-chain-resources-national-emergency-caused-outbreak-
COVID-19/

*President Donald J. Trump Announces Great American
Economic Revival Industry Groups*
https://trumpwhitehouse.archives.gov/briefings-
statements/president-donald-j-trump-announces-great-
american-economic-revival-industry-groups/

*President Donald J. Trump Is Taking Action To Ensure The
Safety Of Our Nation's Food Supply Chain*
https://trumpwhitehouse.archives.gov/briefings-
statements/president-donald-j-trump-taking-action-ensure-
safety-nations-food-supply-chain/

*Remarks by President Trump in Roundtable Discussion with
Industry Executives on Reopening*
https://trumpwhitehouse.archives.gov/briefings-
statements/remarks-president-trump-roundtable-discussion-
industry-executives-reopening/

*President Donald J. Trump Is Working to Secure America's
Seafood Supply Chain and Bring Jobs Home*
https://trumpwhitehouse.archives.gov/briefings-
statements/president-donald-j-trump-working-secure-americas-
seafood-supply-chain-bring-jobs-home/

Reason 38. American Supply Chain Independence

Trump Administration Announces Strategy to Strengthen American Economy
https://www.usgs.gov/news/trump-administration-announces-strategy-strengthen-americas-economy-defense#:~:text=In%202017%2C%20President%20Donald%20Trump,to%20critical%20mineral%20supply%20disruptions.

A Federal Strategy To Ensure Secure and Reliable Supplies of Critical Minerals
https://www.federalregister.gov/documents/2017/12/26/2017-27899/a-federal-strategy-to-ensure-secure-and-reliable-supplies-of-critical-minerals

Reason 39. Real Prison Reform

SECOND CHANCE MONTH, APRIL 2017!
https://trumpwhitehouse.archives.gov/briefings-statements/remarks-president-trump-meeting-prison-reform/

President Donald J. Trump Calls on Congress to Pass the FIRST STEP Act
https://trumpwhitehouse.archives.gov/briefings-statements/president-donald-j-trump-calls-congress-pass-first-step-act/

President Donald J. Trump Is Working to Create a Future of Opportunity and Prosperity for All Americans
https://trumpwhitehouse.archives.gov/briefings-statements/president-donald-j-trump-working-create-future-opportunity-prosperity-americans/

Remarks by President Trump at 2019 Prison Reform Summit and FIRST STEP Act Celebration
https://trumpwhitehouse.archives.gov/briefings-statements/remarks-president-trump-2019-prison-reform-summit-first-step-act-celebration/

President Donald J. Trump Is Helping Americans Gain a Second Chance to Build a Brighter Future
https://trumpwhitehouse.archives.gov/briefings-statements/president-donald-j-trump-helping-americans-gain-second-chance-build-brighter-future/

Proclamation on Second Chance Month, 2019
https://trumpwhitehouse.archives.gov/presidential-actions/proclamation-second-chance-month-2019/

The American Dream is for Everyone!
https://trumpwhitehouse.archives.gov/articles/american-dream-everyone/

Remarks by President Trump on Second Chance Hiring
https://trumpwhitehouse.archives.gov/briefings-statements/remarks-president-trump-second-chance-hiring/

CEA Report: Returns on Investments in Recidivism-Reducing Programs
https://trumpwhitehouse.archives.gov/briefings-statements/cea-report-returns-investments-recidivism-reducing-programs/

President Donald J. Trump Has Championed Reforms That Are Providing Hope to Forgotten Americans
https://trumpwhitehouse.archives.gov/briefings-statements/president-donald-j-trump-championed-reforms-providing-hope-forgotten-americans/

Reason 40. Middle East Peace: Abraham Accords

President Donald J. Trump Has Brokered a Historic Deal Between Israel and the Kingdom of Bahrain
https://trumpwhitehouse.archives.gov/briefings-statements/president-donald-j-trump-brokered-historic-deal-israel-kingdom-bahrain/

The Abraham Accords Declaration
https://trumpwhitehouse.archives.gov/briefings-statements/the-abraham-accords-declaration/

Joint Statement of the United States, the State of Israel, and the United Arab Emirates
https://trumpwhitehouse.archives.gov/briefings-statements/joint-statement-united-states-state-israel-united-arab-emirates/

Peace Through Stability
https://www.theamericanconservative.com/articles/peace-through-stability/

First-ever flight: Plane with US, Israeli officials lands in UAE
https://www.aljazeera.com/news/2020/08/flight-israeli-plane-heads-uae-saudi-arabia-20083107019156.html

THE ABRAHAM ACCORDS DECLARATION
https://trumpwhitehouse.archives.gov/wp-content/uploads/2020/09/ABRAHAM-ACCORDS-DECLARATION.pdf

Abraham Accords: Declaration of Peace, Cooperation, and Constructive Diplomatic and Friendly Relations
https://trumpwhitehouse.archives.gov/briefings-statements/abraham-accords-declaration-peace-cooperation-constructive-diplomatic-friendly-relations/

Remarks by President Trump, Prime Minister Netanyahu, Minister bin Zayed, and Minister Al Zayani at the Abraham Accords Signing Ceremony
https://trumpwhitehouse.archives.gov/briefings-statements/remarks-president-trump-prime-minister-netanyahu-minister-bin-zayed-minister-al-zayani-abraham-accords-signing-ceremony/

Abraham Accords Peace Agreement: Treaty of Peace, Diplomatic Relations and Full Normalization Between the United Arab Emirates and the State of Israel
https://trumpwhitehouse.archives.gov/briefings-statements/abraham-accords-peace-agreement-treaty-of-peace-diplomatic-relations-and-full-normalization-between-the-united-arab-emirates-and-the-state-of-israel/

Reason 41. Cuba

Strengthening the Policy of the United States Toward Cuba
https://www.federalregister.gov/documents/2017/10/20/2017-22928/strengthening-the-policy-of-the-united-states-toward-cuba#:~:text=National%20Security%20Presidential%20Memorandum%20NSPM,heads%20of%20departments%20and%20agencies.

Reason 42. Dealing with China

Proclamation on Suspension of Entry as Immigrants and Nonimmigrants of Persons who Pose a Risk of Transmitting 2019 Novel Coronavirus
https://trumpwhitehouse.archives.gov/presidential-actions/proclamation-suspension-entry-immigrants-nonimmigrants-persons-pose-risk-transmitting-2019-novel-coronavirus/

Readout of President Donald J. Trump's Meeting with President Xi Jinping of China
https://trumpwhitehouse.archives.gov/briefings-statements/readout-president-donald-j-trumps-meeting-president-xi-jinping-china/

The Chinese Communist Party's Ideology and Global Ambitions
https://trumpwhitehouse.archives.gov/briefings-statements/chinese-communist-partys-ideology-global-ambitions/

China's national legislature adopts constitutional amendment
http://www.xinhuanet.com/english/2018-03/11/c_137031606.htm

China Removes Presidential Term Limits, Enabling Xi Jinping To Rule Indefinitely
https://www.npr.org/sections/thetwo-way/2018/03/11/592694991/china-removes-presidential-term-limits-enabling-xi-jinping-to-rule-indefinitely

What's Vladimir Putin's end game? Other post-Soviet autocrats give a few clues.
https://www.washingtonpost.com/politics/2020/07/03/whats-vladimir-putins-end-game-other-post-soviet-autocrats-give-few-clues/

Reason 43. North Korea

Trump Meets Kim at DMZ, Crosses Into North Korea
https://www.voanews.com/usa/trump-meets-kim-dmz-crosses-north-korea

Text of a Notice on the Continuation of the National Emergency With Respect to North Korea
https://trumpwhitehouse.archives.gov/briefings-statements/text-notice-continuation-national-emergency-respect-north-korea/

President Donald J. Trump Has Restored American Leadership On The World Stage
https://trumpwhitehouse.archives.gov/briefings-statements/president-donald-j-trump-restored-american-leadership-world-stage/

Reason 44. A Better KORUS Deal

President Donald J. Trump is Fulfilling His Promise on the United States–Korea Free Trade Agreement and on National Security
https://www.cbp.gov/sites/default/files/assets/documents/2017-Jun/ADCVD%20March%20-%20April%202017%20.pdf

U.S. - Korea Free Trade Agreement
https://ustr.gov/trade-agreements/free-trade-agreements/korus-fta

Reason 45. The Iran Deal

Imposing Sanctions With Respect to Iran
https://www.federalregister.gov/documents/2019/06/26/2019-13793/imposing-sanctions-with-respect-to-iran

Remarks by President Trump on Proposed National Environmental Policy Act Regulations
https://trumpwhitehouse.archives.gov/briefings-statements/remarks-president-trump-proposed-national-environmental-policy-act-regulations/

Reason 46. Trans-Pacific Partnership

Presidential Memorandum Regarding Withdrawal of the United States from the Trans-Pacific Partnership Negotiations and Agreement
https://trumpwhitehouse.archives.gov/presidential-actions/presidential-memorandum-regarding-withdrawal-united-states-trans-pacific-partnership-negotiations-agreement/

Reason 47. Paris Climate Accord

President Trump Puts American Jobs First
https://trumpwhitehouse.archives.gov/briefings-statements/president-trump-puts-american-jobs-first/

President Trump Announces U.S. Withdrawal From the Paris Climate Accord
https://trumpwhitehouse.archives.gov/articles/president-trump-announces-u-s-withdrawal-paris-climate-accord/

Statement by President Trump on the Paris Climate Accord
https://trumpwhitehouse.archives.gov/briefings-statements/statement-president-trump-paris-climate-accord/

Reason 48. Empowering Women

NASA GIRLS and NASA BOYS
https://women.nasa.gov/nasagirls/

H.R.255 - Promoting Women in Entrepreneurship Act
https://www.congress.gov/bill/115th-congress/house-bill/255

H.R.321 - Inspiring the Next Space Pioneers, Innovators, Researchers, and Explorers (INSPIRE) Women Act
https://www.congress.gov/bill/115th-congress/house-bill/321

S.3247 - Women's Entrepreneurship and Economic Empowerment Act of 2018
https://www.congress.gov/bill/115th-congress/senate-bill/3247

Reason 49. STEM

H.R.4254 - Women in Aerospace Education Act
https://www.congress.gov/bill/115th-congress/house-bill/4254

Amazon, Facebook and others in tech will commit $300 million to the White House's new computer science push
https://www.vox.com/2017/9/26/16364662/amazon-facebook-google-tech-300-million-donald-trump-ivanka-computer-science

Reason 50. Remembering Suffrage

Readout from the Launch of the "Building the Movement Exhibit: America's Youth Celebrate 100 Years of Women's Suffrage"
https://trumpwhitehouse.archives.gov/briefings-statements/readout-launch-building-movement-exhibit-americas-youth-celebrate-100-years-womens-suffrage/

Reason 51. Education and School Choice

Executive Order on Improving Free Inquiry, Transparency, and Accountability at Colleges and Universities
https://trumpwhitehouse.archives.gov/presidential-actions/executive-order-improving-free-inquiry-transparency-accountability-colleges-universities/

Marking a Milestone for School Choice

174

https://trumpwhitehouse.archives.gov/articles/marking-milestone-school-choice/

Remarks by President Trump at a Roundtable on Empowering Families with Education Choice
https://trumpwhitehouse.archives.gov/briefings-statements/remarks-president-trump-roundtable-empowering-families-education-choice/

President Trump Is Fighting For Every Family's Freedom To Choose The Best Possible Education For Their Children
https://trumpwhitehouse.archives.gov/briefings-statements/president-trump-is-fighting-for-every-familys-freedom-to-choose-the-best-possible-education-for-their-children/

S.634 - Education Freedom Scholarships and Opportunity Act
https://www.congress.gov/bill/116th-congress/senate-bill/634#:~:text=%2F28%2F2019)-,Education%20Freedom%20Scholarships%20and%20Opportunity%20Act,tax%20credit%20under%20this%20bill

Remarks by President Trump at Parent-Teacher Conference Listening Session
https://trumpwhitehouse.archives.gov/briefings-statements/remarks-president-trump-parent-teacher-conference-listening-session/

Remarks by President Trump in Parent-Teacher Conference Listening Session
https://trumpwhitehouse.archives.gov/briefings-statements/remarks-president-trump-parent-teacher-conference-listening-session-2/

Memorandum on Continued Student Loan Payment Relief During the COVID-19 Pandemic
https://trumpwhitehouse.archives.gov/presidential-actions/memorandum-continued-student-loan-payment-relief-COVID-19-pandemic/

Reason 52. Smarter FDA Practices

Coronavirus (COVID-19) Update: FDA Issues First Emergency Authorization for Sample Pooling in Diagnostic Testing
https://www.fda.gov/news-events/press-announcements/coronavirus-covid-19-update-fda-issues-first-emergency-authorization-sample-pooling-diagnostic

H.R.4374 - To amend the Federal Food, Drug, and Cosmetic Act to authorize additional emergency uses for medical products to reduce deaths and severity of injuries caused by agents of war, and for other purposes.
https://www.congress.gov/bill/115th-congress/house-bill/4374/text

Reason 53. Auto Industry Revival

The US auto industry may surprise everyone in 2017
https://www.businessinsider.com/us-auto-industry-growth-in-2017-2016-12

General Motors says to invest additional $1 billion in U.S.
https://www.reuters.com/article/us-gm-jobs-trump/general-motors-says-to-invest-additional-1-billion-in-u-s-idUSKBN15107B

Hyundai Boosts U.S. Investment to $3.1 Billion After Trump's Threats
https://fortune.com/2017/01/17/donald-trump-hyundai-auto-investment/

Toyota to invest $10 billion in U.S. over five years
https://www.reuters.com/article/us-usa-autoshow-toyota/toyota-to-invest-10-billion-in-u-s-over-five-years-idUSKBN14T1NN

Toyota announces plans to invest $600 million, add 400 jobs to Indiana plant
https://www.japantimes.co.jp/news/2017/01/25/business/corporate-business/without-mentioning-trump-toyota-announces-plans-invest-600-million-add-400-jobs-indiana-plant/

Which manufacturers are bringing the most jobs back to America?
https://www.usatoday.com/story/money/business/2018/06/28/manufacturers-bringing-most-jobs-back-to-america/36438051/

Reason 54. Better Trade Fairness

Remarks by President Trump in Listening Session with Representatives from the Steel and Aluminum Industry
https://trumpwhitehouse.archives.gov/briefings-statements/remarks-president-trump-listening-session-representatives-steel-aluminum-industry/

President Donald J. Trump Has Forged New Trade Agreements to Revitalize American Industry and Agriculture
https://trumpwhitehouse.archives.gov/briefings-statements/president-donald-j-trump-forged-new-trade-agreements-revitalize-american-industry/

Memorandum on Steel Imports and Threats to National Security
https://www.govinfo.gov/content/pkg/DCPD-
201700259/pdf/DCPD-201700259.pdf

Presidential Proclamation on Adjusting Imports of Aluminum into the United States
https://trumpwhitehouse.archives.gov/presidential-
actions/presidential-proclamation-adjusting-imports-aluminum-
united-states/

Reason 55. U.S. Worker Force

Pledge to America's Workers
https://trumpwhitehouse.archives.gov/pledge-to-americas-
workers/

Reinvesting in the American Workforce
https://trumpwhitehouse.archives.gov/articles/reinvesting-
american-workforce/

Remarks by President Trump at Prison Reform Roundtable
https://trumpwhitehouse.archives.gov/briefings-
statements/remarks-president-trump-prison-reform-roundtable/

Executive Order Establishing the President's National Council for the American Worker
https://trumpwhitehouse.archives.gov/presidential-
actions/executive-order-establishing-presidents-national-
council-american-worker/

Continuing the President's National Council for the American Worker and the American Workforce Policy Advisory Board
https://www.federalregister.gov/documents/2020/07/01/2020-
14328/continuing-the-presidents-national-council-for-the-
american-worker-and-the-american-workforce-policy

Reason 56. Supporting Farmers and Agriculture

H.R.439 - National FFA Organization's Federal Charter Amendments Act
https://www.congress.gov/bill/116th-congress/house-bill/439

Agriculture Tax Reform Listening Session
https://trumpwhitehouse.archives.gov/articles/agriculture-tax-reform-listening-session/

President Donald J. Trump is Protecting America's Farmers Against Unfair and Retaliatory Trade Practices
https://trumpwhitehouse.archives.gov/briefings-statements/president-donald-j-trump-protecting-americas-farmers-unfair-retaliatory-trade-practices/

BIO President: Executive Order on Agricultural Biotechnology Is 'Important Step Forward'
https://www.bio.org/press-release/bio-president-executive-order-agricultural-biotechnology-%E2%80%98important-step-forward%E2%80%99

WTAS: Support for President Donald J. Trump's Plan to Protect American Farmers from Unjustified Trade Retaliation
https://trumpwhitehouse.archives.gov/briefings-statements/wtas-support-president-donald-j-trumps-plan-protect-american-farmers-unjustified-trade-retaliation/

Estate Tax Repeal
https://www.fb.org/issues/tax-reform/estate-tax-repeal/

H. R. 1
https://www.congress.gov/115/bills/hr1/BILLS-115hr1enr.pdf

H.R.5422 - Death Tax Repeal Act
https://www.congress.gov/bill/115th-congress/house-bill/5422

S.215 - Death Tax Repeal Act of 2019
https://www.congress.gov/bill/116th-congress/senate-bill/215?s=1&r=40

Remarks by President Trump at the 91st Annual Future Farmers of America Convention and Expo
https://trumpwhitehouse.archives.gov/briefings-statements/remarks-president-trump-91st-annual-future-farmers-america-convention-expo/

WTAS: Support for President Donald J. Trump's Plan to Protect American Farmers from Unjustified Trade Retaliation
https://trumpwhitehouse.archives.gov/briefings-statements/wtas-support-president-donald-j-trumps-plan-protect-american-farmers-unjustified-trade-retaliation/

Trump Administration Stands Behind Ag Producers
https://trumpwhitehouse.archives.gov/articles/trump-administration-stands-behind-ag-producers/

H.R.5422 - Death Tax Repeal Act
https://www.congress.gov/bill/115th-congress/house-bill/5422

S.215 - Death Tax Repeal Act of 2019
https://www.congress.gov/bill/116th-congress/senate-bill/215?s=1&r=40

Under Secretary Northey: "The USMCA Is a 'Big Win' for Iowa's Agriculture Industry"
https://trumpwhitehouse.archives.gov/briefings-statements/secretary-northey-usmca-big-win-iowas-agriculture-industry/

Agriculture Tax Reform Listening Session
https://trumpwhitehouse.archives.gov/articles/agriculture-tax-reform-listening-session/

Remarks by President Trump to the American Farm Bureau Annual Convention
https://trumpwhitehouse.archives.gov/briefings-statements/remarks-president-trump-american-farm-bureau-annual-convention-nashville-tn/

Remarks by President Trump at the American Farm Bureau Federation Annual Convention and Trade Show
https://trumpwhitehouse.archives.gov/briefings-statements/remarks-president-trump-american-farm-bureau-federation-annual-convention-trade-show/

USMCA Keeps Illinois Farmers Leading the Pack
https://trumpwhitehouse.archives.gov/articles/usmca-keeps-illinois-farmers-leading-pack/

Presidential Proclamation on National School Lunch Week, 2019
https://trumpwhitehouse.archives.gov/presidential-actions/presidential-proclamation-national-school-lunch-week-2019/

Reason 57. Supporting U.S. Ranchers

China buying more US beef and soybeans
https://www.agri-pulse.com/articles/13545-china-buying-more-us-beef-and-soybeans
https://ustr.gov/about-us/policy-offices/press-office/press-releases/2020/august/joint-statement-united-states-and-european-union-tariff-agreement

Livestock, Dairy, and Poultry Outlook
https://www.ers.usda.gov/webdocs/outlooks/99169/ldp-m-314.pdf?v=7583.3

Remarks by President Trump at Signing of a U.S.-EU Trade Agreement
https://trumpwhitehouse.archives.gov/briefings-statements/remarks-president-trump-signing-u-s-eu-trade-agreement/

U.S. Beef Exports By Country (Year-to-Date)
https://beef2live.com/story-beef-exports-country-year-date-0-109756

USDA Economic Research Service United States Department of Agriculture
https://www.ers.usda.gov/

Livestock, Dairy, and Poultry Outlook
https://www.ers.usda.gov/webdocs/outlooks/99169/ldp-m-314.pdf?v=7583.3

US beef exports soar to a record in 2018, but China growth remains elusive
https://www.cnbc.com/2019/03/08/us-beef-exports-soar-to-record-in-2018-but-china-growth-still-elusive.html

Remarks by President Trump on Supporting America's Farmers and Ranchers
https://trumpwhitehouse.archives.gov/briefings-statements/remarks-president-trump-supporting-americas-farmers-ranchers/

MT's "Great Falls Tribune" Praises President Trump's Beef Export Deal With China
https://trumpwhitehouse.archives.gov/briefings-statements/icymi-mts-great-falls-tribune-praises-president-trumps-beef-export-deal-china/

Remarks by President Trump on Supporting our Nation's Farmers, Ranchers, and Food Supply Chain
https://trumpwhitehouse.archives.gov/briefings-statements/remarks-president-trump-supporting-nations-farmers-ranchers-food-supply-chain/

Presidential Proclamation on National School Lunch Week, 2019
https://trumpwhitehouse.archives.gov/presidential-actions/presidential-proclamation-national-school-lunch-week-2019/

UNITED STATES–MEXICO–CANADA TRADE FACT SHEET Agriculture: Market Access and Dairy Outcomes of the USMC Agreement
https://ustr.gov/trade-agreements/free-trade-agreements/united-states-mexico-canada-agreement/fact-sheets/market-access-and-dairy-outcomes

Trump's deal with Mexico and Canada is welcome news for American pork producers hit by US-China trade war
https://www.cnbc.com/2019/05/17/us-deal-with-canada-mexico-welcome-news-for-american-pork-industry.html

Japan ends longstanding trade restrictions on American beef, setting stage for exports to grow
https://www.cnbc.com/2019/05/17/japan-ends-longstanding-trade-restrictions-on-american-beef-usda.html

Trump Announces a Trade Pact With Japan
https://www.nytimes.com/2019/09/25/business/trump-announces-limited-trade-pact-with-japan.html

US, Japan sign trade deal to lower tariffs on agricultural goods
https://www.fooddive.com/news/how-the-us-and-japan-trade-deal-could-help-farmers/563721/

Reason 58. U.S. Fishing

President Donald J. Trump Signs H.R. 374, H.R. 510, H.R. 873, and H.R. 2430 into Law
https://trumpwhitehouse.archives.gov/briefings-statements/president-donald-j-trump-signs-h-r-374-h-r-510-h-r-873-h-r-2430-law/

Memorandum on Protecting the United States Lobster Industry
https://trumpwhitehouse.archives.gov/presidential-actions/memorandum-protecting-united-states-lobster-industry/

Executive Order on Promoting American Seafood Competitiveness and Economic Growth
https://trumpwhitehouse.archives.gov/presidential-actions/executive-order-promoting-american-seafood-competitiveness-economic-growth/

Remarks By President Trump In A Roundtable On Supporting America's Commercial Fishermen
https://trumpwhitehouse.archives.gov/briefings-statements/remarks-president-trump-roundtable-supporting-americas-commercial-fishermen/

President Donald J. Trump Is Working to Secure America's Seafood Supply Chain and Bring Jobs Home
https://trumpwhitehouse.archives.gov/briefings-statements/president-donald-j-trump-working-secure-americas-seafood-supply-chain-bring-jobs-home/

Proclamation on Modifying The Northeast Canyons And Seamounts Marine National Monument
https://trumpwhitehouse.archives.gov/presidential-actions/proclamation-modifying-northeast-canyons-seamounts-marine-national-monument/

Modifying the Northeast Canyons and Seamounts Marine National Monument
https://www.federalregister.gov/documents/2020/06/11/2020-12823/modifying-the-northeast-canyons-and-seamounts-marine-national-monument

Reason 59. Rural Broadband

Improving Rural Health and Telehealth Access
https://www.federalregister.gov/documents/2020/08/06/2020-17364/improving-rural-health-and-telehealth-access

Supporting Broadband Tower Facilities in Rural America on Federal Properties Managed by the Department of the Interior
https://www.federalregister.gov/documents/2018/01/12/2018-00628/supporting-broadband-tower-facilities-in-rural-america-on-federal-properties-managed-by-the

Executive Order on An America-First Healthcare Plan
https://trumpwhitehouse.archives.gov/presidential-actions/executive-order-america-first-healthcare-plan/

Reason 60. The Economy

Readout of President Donald J. Trump's National Economic Council Listening Session
https://trumpwhitehouse.archives.gov/briefings-statements/readout-president-donald-j-trumps-national-economic-council-listening-session/

The Historic Results Of President Donald J. Trump's Economic Agenda
https://trumpwhitehouse.archives.gov/briefings-statements/historic-results-president-donald-j-trumps-economic-agenda/

Restoring the Rule of Law, Federalism, and Economic Growth by Reviewing the "Waters of the United States" Rule
https://www.federalregister.gov/documents/2017/03/03/2017-04353/restoring-the-rule-of-law-federalism-and-economic-growth-by-reviewing-the-waters-of-the-united

Executive Order 13783: Promoting Energy Independence and Economic Growth
https://www.epa.gov/sites/production/files/2017-10/documents/memo_eo13783_energy_independence_economic_growth.pdf

Buy American and Hire American
https://www.federalregister.gov/documents/2017/04/21/2017-08311/buy-american-and-hire-american

President Donald J. Trump Announces Great American Economic Revival Industry Groups
https://trumpwhitehouse.archives.gov/briefings-statements/president-donald-j-trump-announces-great-american-economic-revival-industry-groups/

Reason 61. Elder Care

President Donald J. Trump Signs S. 178, S. 652, and H.R. 1117 into Law; Elder Abuse Prevention and Prosecution Act
https://trumpwhitehouse.archives.gov/briefings-statements/president-donald-j-trump-signs-s-178-s-652-h-r-1117-law/

Remarks by President Trump in Roundtable Discussion on Fighting for America's Seniors
https://trumpwhitehouse.archives.gov/briefings-statements/remarks-president-trump-roundtable-discussion-fighting-americas-seniors/

Executive Order on Lowering Prices for Patients by Eliminating Kickbacks to Middlemen
https://trumpwhitehouse.archives.gov/presidential-actions/executive-order-lowering-prices-patients-eliminating-kickbacks-middlemen/

Increasing Drug Importation To Lower Prices for American Patients
https://www.federalregister.gov/documents/2020/07/29/2020-16624/increasing-drug-importation-to-lower-prices-for-american-patients

Combating Public Health Emergencies and Strengthening National Security by Ensuring Essential Medicines, Medical Countermeasures, and Critical Inputs Are Made in the United States
https://www.federalregister.gov/documents/2020/08/14/2020-18012/combating-public-health-emergencies-and-strengthening-national-security-by-ensuring-essential

President Donald J. Trump Is Taking Strong Action to Further Protect Nursing Homes from the Coronavirus
https://trumpwhitehouse.archives.gov/briefings-statements/president-donald-j-trump-is-taking-decisive-action-to-protect-vulnerable-citizens-in-americas-nursing-homes/

Reason 62. African American History

H.R.1927 - African American Civil Rights Network Act of 2017
https://www.congress.gov/bill/115th-congress/house-bill/1927

H.R.2989 - Frederick Douglass Bicentennial Commission Act
https://www.congress.gov/bill/115th-congress/house-bill/2989

Presidential Message on the 55th Anniversary of the Civil Rights Act of 1964

https://trumpwhitehouse.archives.gov/briefings-
statements/presidential-message-55th-anniversary-civil-rights-
act-1964/

*S.3191 - Civil Rights Cold Case Records Collection Act of
2018*
https://www.congress.gov/bill/115th-congress/senate-bill/3191

Reason 63. Addressing DACA

*White House Framework on Immigration Reform & Border
Security*
https://trumpwhitehouse.archives.gov/briefings-
statements/white-house-framework-immigration-reform-
border-security/

Reason 64. State Support

Lack Of Controlled Burns Contributing To California Wildfires
https://sanfrancisco.cbslocal.com/2018/08/03/lack-of-
controlled-burns-contributing-to-california-wildfires/

Disaster Relief:
https://trumpwhitehouse.archives.gov/briefings-
statements/president-donald-j-trump-approves-california-
disaster-declaration-082220/

https://trumpwhitehouse.archives.gov/briefings-
statements/president-donald-j-trump-approves-oregon-disaster-
declaration-091520/

https://trumpwhitehouse.archives.gov/briefings-
statements/president-donald-j-trump-approves-louisiana-
disaster-declaration-082920/

S. 496 (115th): A bill to repeal the rule issued by the Federal Highway Administration and the Federal Transit Administration entitled "Metropolitan Planning Organization Coordination and Planning Area Reform".
https://www.govtrack.us/congress/bills/115/s496/summary

Enforcing Statutory Prohibitions on Federal Control of Education
https://www.federalregister.gov/documents/2017/05/01/2017-08905/enforcing-statutory-prohibitions-on-federal-control-of-education

Remarks by President Trump to the Nation's Mayors on Transforming America's Communities
https://trumpwhitehouse.archives.gov/briefings-statements/remarks-president-trump-nations-mayors-transforming-americas-communities/

Remarks by President Trump at Working Session with Mayors
https://trumpwhitehouse.archives.gov/briefings-statements/remarks-president-trump-working-session-mayors/

CALFIRE
https://www.fire.ca.gov/incidents/

US West Coast fires: Is Trump right to blame forest management?
https://www.bbc.com/news/world-us-canada-46183690

California's government solely responsible for states forest management and wildfire debacle
https://wattsupwiththat.com/2019/05/14/californias-government-solely-responsible-for-states-forest-management-and-wildfire-debacle/

Fire on the Mountain: Rethinking Forest Management in the Sierra Nevada
https://lhc.ca.gov/report/fire-mountain-rethinking-forest-management-sierra-nevada

President Donald J. Trump Approves California Disaster Declaration
https://trumpwhitehouse.archives.gov/briefings-statements/president-donald-j-trump-approves-california-disaster-declaration-2/

President Donald J. Trump Approves California Disaster Declaration
https://trumpwhitehouse.archives.gov/briefings-statements/president-donald-j-trump-approves-california-disaster-declaration-3/

President Donald J. Trump's Administration Is Providing Support to Fight the California Wildfires and Help Those Affected
https://trumpwhitehouse.archives.gov/briefings-statements/president-donald-j-trumps-administration-providing-support-fight-california-wildfires-help-affected/

DCPD-201800866 - Executive Order 13855-Promoting Active Management of America's Forests, Rangelands, and Other Federal Lands To Improve Conditions and Reduce Wildfire Risk
https://www.govinfo.gov/app/details/DCPD-201800866

ORDER NO. 3372
https://www.blm.gov/sites/blm.gov/files/SO%203372.pdf

EO on Promoting Active Management of America's Forests, Rangelands, and other Federal Lands to Improve Conditions and Reduce Wildfire Risk
https://trumpwhitehouse.archives.gov/presidential-actions/eo-promoting-active-management-americas-forests-rangelands-federal-lands-improve-conditions-reduce-wildfire-risk/

Reason 65. Fighting Human Trafficking

Remarks by President Trump at Listening Session on Domestic and International Human Trafficking
https://trumpwhitehouse.archives.gov/briefings-statements/remarks-president-trump-listening-session-domestic-international-human-trafficking/

H.R.2200 - Frederick Douglass Trafficking Victims Prevention and Protection Reauthorization Act of 2018
https://www.congress.gov/bill/115th-congress/house-bill/2200/text

Issuance of Permits With Respect to Facilities and Land Transportation Crossings at the International Boundaries of the United States
https://www.federalregister.gov/documents/2019/04/15/2019-07645/issuance-of-permits-with-respect-to-facilities-and-land-transportation-crossings-at-the

Combating Human Trafficking and Online Child Exploitation in the United States
https://www.federalregister.gov/documents/2020/02/05/2020-02438/combating-human-trafficking-and-online-child-exploitation-in-the-united-states

Reason 66. Protecting the Environment

Ocean Policy To Advance the Economic, Security, and Environmental Interests of the United States
https://www.federalregister.gov/documents/2018/06/22/2018-13640/ocean-policy-to-advance-the-economic-security-and-environmental-interests-of-the-united-states

EO 13766: Expediting Environmental Reviews and Approvals for High Priority Infrastructure Projects (2017)
https://www.energy.gov/nepa/downloads/eo-13766-expediting-environmental-reviews-and-approvals-high-priority-infrastructure

DCPD-201700065 - Executive Order 13766-Expediting Environmental Reviews and Approvals for High-Priority Infrastructure Projects
https://www.govinfo.gov/app/details/DCPD-201700065

S.483 - Pesticide Registration Improvement Extension Act of 2018
https://www.congress.gov/bill/116th-congress/senate-bill/483

S.47 - John D. Dingell, Jr. Conservation, Management, and Recreation Act
https://www.congress.gov/bill/116th-congress/senate-bill/47

President Donald J. Trump Is Conserving and Restoring the Majesty of America's Public Lands
https://trumpwhitehouse.archives.gov/briefings-statements/president-donald-j-trump-conserving-restoring-majesty-americas-public-lands/

Reason 67. U.S. Parks

S.3422 - Great American Outdoors Act
https://www.congress.gov/bill/116th-congress/senate-bill/3422

President Trump Signs the Great American Outdoors Act, Preserving and Protecting our National Parks
https://trumpwhitehouse.archives.gov/articles/president-trump-signs-great-american-outdoors-act-preserving-protecting-national-parks/

Trump Donates First-Quarter Salary to National Park Service
https://www.nytimes.com/2017/04/03/us/politics/national-park-service-trump-salary.html

3 U.S. Code § 102 - Compensation of the President
https://www.law.cornell.edu/uscode/text/3/102

Camp Nelson: In the Footsteps of Freedom
https://www.nps.gov/cane/index.htm

Camp Nelson
https://www.nps.gov/cane/learn/historyculture/index.htm

Reason 68. Foreign Terrorism

S.1595 - Hizballah International Financing Prevention Amendments Act of 2018
https://www.congress.gov/bill/115th-congress/senate-bill/1595

Executive Order 13823—Protecting America Through Lawful Detention of Terrorists
https://www.presidency.ucsb.edu/documents/executive-order-13823-protecting-america-through-lawful-detention-terrorists

Executive Order 13780: Protecting the Nation From Foreign Terrorist Entry Into the United States Initial Section 11 Report
https://www.dhs.gov/publication/executive-order-13780-protecting-nation-foreign-terrorist-entry-united-states-initial

Trump Eliminates Some Of World's Top Terrorists In Just A Few Months
https://dailycaller.com/2020/01/03/trump-terrorists-soleimani-baghdadi-killed/

Reason 69. Protecting America

DCPD-201900176 - Executive Order 13865-Coordinating National Resilience to Electromagnetic Pulses
https://www.govinfo.gov/app/details/DCPD-201900176

Securing the Information and Communications Technology and Services Supply Chain
https://www.federalregister.gov/documents/2019/05/17/2019-10538/securing-the-information-and-communications-technology-and-services-supply-chain

Coordinating National Resilience to Electromagnetic Pulses
https://www.federalregister.gov/documents/2019/03/29/2019-06325/coordinating-national-resilience-to-electromagnetic-pulses

Reason 70. Drug-Free Youth

ONDCP's Drug-Free Communities Program Highlights Trump Administration Success in Lowering Youth Substance Use
https://trumpwhitehouse.archives.gov/briefings-statements/ondcps-drug-free-communities-program-highlights-trump-administration-success-lowering-youth-substance-use/

President Trump Awards an Historic Number of DFC Grants to Prevent Youth Substance Use
https://trumpwhitehouse.archives.gov/briefings-statements/president-trump-awards-historic-number-dfc-grants-prevent-youth-substance-use/

194

ONDCP Announces New Grant Applications for Drug-Free Communities Program
https://trumpwhitehouse.archives.gov/briefings-statements/ondcp-announces-new-grant-applications-drug-free-communities-program/

Trump Administration Announces First Phase of FY 2020 Drug-Free Communities Grants Awards to Community Coalitions Across the Country
https://trumpwhitehouse.archives.gov/briefings-statements/trump-administration-announces-first-phase-fy-2020-drug-free-communities-grants-awards-community-coalitions-across-country/

Drug-Free Communities Support Program National Evaluation ANNUAL REPORT JULY 2020
https://trumpwhitehouse.archives.gov/wp-content/uploads/2020/07/2020-ONDCP-DFC-Evaluation-Report.pdf

Drug-Free Communities Support Program National Evaluation EXECUTIVE SUMMARY JULY 2020
https://trumpwhitehouse.archives.gov/wp-content/uploads/2020/07/2020-ONDCP-DFC-Evaluation-Report_Executive-Summary.pdf

Reason 71. Government Shutdown 2018/19

The government shutdown is in day 35 and has shattered the record for the longest shutdown in history
https://www.businessinsider.com/history-of-government-shutdowns-in-congress-2018-1

Reason 72. Supporting Law Enforcement

S.998 - Supporting and Treating Officers In Crisis Act of 2019
https://www.congress.gov/bill/116th-congress/senate-
bill/998/text

Safe Policing for Safe Communities
https://www.federalregister.gov/documents/2020/06/19/2020-
13449/safe-policing-for-safe-communities

Remarks by President Trump in Listening Session with the Fraternal Order of Police
https://trumpwhitehouse.archives.gov/briefings-
statements/remarks-president-trump-listening-session-fraternal-
order-police/

Fraternal Order of Police endorses Trump, including lodge in Biden's home state
https://justthenews.com/politics-policy/all-things-
trump/fraternal-order-police-endorse-trump-including-lodge-
bidens-home

Fraternal Order of Police Endorses Trump as President Positions Himself as the Law and Order Candidate
https://www.newsweek.com/fraternal-order-police-endorses-
trump-president-positions-himself-law-order-candidate-
1529785

Delaware Fraternal Order of Police endorses Trump; president responds
https://www.delawareonline.com/story/news/2020/09/05/delaw
are-fraternal-order-of-police-endorses-trump-president-
responds/5728007002/

Largest police union endorses Trump for reelection
https://thehill.com/homenews/campaign/515110-largest-police-
union-endorses-trump-for-re-election

Chicago police union endorses President Trump's reelection bid
https://www.chicagotribune.com/politics/ct-chicago-fop-endorses-trump-20200909-ygzku56tpvgp5amr76z7txu74u-story.html

President Donald J. Trump Is Taking Unprecedented Steps To Strengthen Relations Between Law Enforcement And Their Communities
https://trumpwhitehouse.archives.gov/briefings-statements/president-donald-j-trump-taking-unprecedented-steps-strengthen-relations-law-enforcement-communities/

PROJECT SAFE NEIGHBORHOODS
https://www.justice.gov/psn

Project Safe Neighborhoods (PSN)
https://bja.ojp.gov/program/project-safe-neighborhoods-psn/overview

PRESIDENTIAL COMMISSION ON LAW ENFORCEMENT AND THE ADMINISTRATION OF JUSTICE
https://www.justice.gov/ag/presidential-commission-law-enforcement-and-administration-justice

Reason 73. Pardons, Commutations & Clemencies

Statement from the Press Secretary Regarding Executive Clemency for Patrick Nolan
https://trumpwhitehouse.archives.gov/briefings-statements/statement-press-secretary-regarding-executive-clemency-patrick-nolan/

Statement from the Press Secretary Regarding Executive Grants of Clemency
https://trumpwhitehouse.archives.gov/briefings-statements/statement-press-secretary-regarding-executive-grants-clemency/

Statement from the Press Secretary Regarding Executive Grants of Clemency
https://trumpwhitehouse.archives.gov/briefings-statements/statement-press-secretary-regarding-executive-grants-clemency-2/

President Trump Pardons Sheriff Joe Arpaio
https://trumpwhitehouse.archives.gov/briefings-statements/president-trump-pardons-sheriff-joe-arpaio/

Remarks by President Trump Granting a Full Pardon to Alice Johnson
https://trumpwhitehouse.archives.gov/briefings-statements/remarks-president-trump-granting-full-pardon-alice-johnson/

Alice Johnson, pardoned by Trump, was put away for life under Biden-sponsored bill
https://nypost.com/2020/08/27/ex-con-pardoned-by-trump-was-put-away-by-bidens-crime-bill/

What to Know About Alice Marie Johnson, the Prison Reform Advocate Who Was Freed From a Life Sentence
https://www.harpersbazaar.com/celebrity/latest/a20968667/who-is-alice-marie-johnson-kim-kardashian-prison-reform/

Statement from the Press Secretary Regarding the Pardon of Susan B. Anthony
https://trumpwhitehouse.archives.gov/briefings-statements/statement-press-secretary-regarding-pardon-susan-b-anthony/

Statement from the Press Secretary Regarding the Pardon of I. "Scooter" Lewis Libby
https://trumpwhitehouse.archives.gov/briefings-statements/statement-press-secretary-regarding-pardon-scooter-lewis-libby/

Statement from the Press Secretary Regarding the Pardon of Dinesh D'Souza
https://trumpwhitehouse.archives.gov/briefings-statements/statement-press-secretary-regarding-pardon-dinesh-dsouza/

Remarks by President Trump at Pardoning of John Arthur "Jack" Johnson
https://trumpwhitehouse.archives.gov/briefings-statements/remarks-president-trump-pardoning-john-arthur-jack-johnson/

Statement from the Press Secretary Regarding Executive Clemency for Michael Behenna
https://trumpwhitehouse.archives.gov/briefings-statements/statement-press-secretary-regarding-executive-clemency-michael-behenna/

Reason 74. Return of Prisoners and POW Remains

Trump Greets 3 American Detainees Freed From North Korea
https://www.nytimes.com/2018/05/10/us/politics/trump-korea-detainees-pompeo.html

WTAS: The Trump Administration Secures the Release of Three Americans from North Korea
https://trumpwhitehouse.archives.gov/briefings-statements/wtas-trump-administration-secures-release-three-americans-north-korea/

Statement by President Donald J. Trump on the Passing of Otto Warmbier
https://trumpwhitehouse.archives.gov/briefings-statements/statement-president-donald-j-trump-passing-otto-warmbier/

Reason 75. Standing up for the U.S. at the UN

Remarks by President Trump to the 75th Session of the United Nations General Assembly
https://trumpwhitehouse.archives.gov/briefings-statements/remarks-president-trump-75th-session-united-nations-general-assembly/

Remarks by President Trump to the 74th Session of the United Nations General Assembly
https://trumpwhitehouse.archives.gov/briefings-statements/remarks-president-trump-74th-session-united-nations-general-assembly/

Reason 76. Renewable Energy

The Trump Administration Is Advancing Clean, Reliable, and Affordable Hydropower
https://trumpwhitehouse.archives.gov/articles/trump-administration-advancing-clean-reliable-affordable-hydropower/

Reason 77. Banks Give Back

Remarks by President Trump in National Economic Council Listening Session with CEOs of Small and Community Banks
https://trumpwhitehouse.archives.gov/briefings-statements/remarks-president-trump-national-economic-council-listening-session-ceos-small-community-banks/
200

JPMorgan Chase Makes Long-Term U.S. Investment in Employees, Branch Expansion and Local Economic Growth
https://www.jpmorganchase.com/corporate/news/pr/multi-billion-investment-employees-local-economies.htm

Reason 78. Foreign Investing in U.S.

42 South Korean companies to invest $17bn in US by 2021
https://asia.nikkei.com/Economy/42-South-Korean-companies-to-invest-17bn-in-US-by-20212

SK Innovation Acquires Dow Chemical's Ethylene Acrylic Acid Unit
http://www.businesskorea.co.kr/news/articleView.html?idxno=17203

After Meeting Trump, Japanese Mogul Pledges $50 Billion Investment in the U.S.
https://www.nytimes.com/2016/12/06/business/dealbook/donald-trump-mayayoshi-son-softbank.html

SoftBank's Masayoshi Son Promised Trump He'd Invest $50 Billion And Create 50,000 U.S. Jobs. Did He Deliver?
https://www.forbes.com/sites/bizcarson/2019/12/10/softbank-masayoshi-son-job-promise-president-donald-trump-progress/

Reason 79. Small Businesses

Remarks by the Vice President in a Listening Session with Small Business Owners
https://trumpwhitehouse.archives.gov/briefings-statements/remarks-vice-president-listening-session-small-business-owners/

S.97 - Nuclear Energy Innovation Capabilities Act of 2017
https://www.congress.gov/bill/115th-congress/senate-bill/97

H.R.6758 - SUCCESS Act
https://www.congress.gov/bill/115th-congress/house-bill/6758/text

Reason 80. The WTO

US - President signs Executive Order establishing Office of Trade and Manufacturing Policy
https://www.internationaltradecomplianceupdate.com/2017/05/05/us-president-signs-executive-order-establishing-office-of-trade-and-manufacturing-policy/

DCPD-201700300 - Executive Order 13797-Establishment of Office of Trade and Manufacturing Policy
https://www.govinfo.gov/app/details/DCPD-201700300

Executive Order 10582--Prescribing uniform procedures for certain determinations under the Buy-American Act
https://www.archives.gov/federal-register/codification/executive-order/10582.html

DEPARTMENT OF DEFENSE GENERAL SERVICES ADMINISTRATION NATIONAL AERONAUTICS AND SPACE ADMINISTRATION
https://www.govinfo.gov/content/pkg/FR-2020-09-14/html/2020-20116.htm

Executive Order on Maximizing Use of American-Made Goods, Products, and Materials
https://trumpwhitehouse.archives.gov/presidential-actions/executive-order-maximizing-use-american-made-goods-products-materials/

202

Executive Order 13797—Establishment of Office of Trade and Manufacturing Policy
https://www.presidency.ucsb.edu/documents/executive-order-13797-establishment-office-trade-and-manufacturing-policy

Reforming Developing-Country Status in the World Trade Organization
https://www.federalregister.gov/documents/2019/07/31/2019-16497/reforming-developing-country-status-in-the-world-trade-organization

Request for Comments Concerning China's Compliance With World Trade Organization (WTO) Commitments
https://www.federalregistcr.gov/documents/2020/08/18/2020-18011/request-for-comments-concerning-chinas-compliance-with-world-trade-organization-wto-commitments

Request for Comments and Notice of Public Hearing Concerning Russia's Implementation of Its WTO Commitments
https://www.federalregister.gov/documents/2020/08/13/2020-17662/request-for-comments-and-notice-of-public-hearing-concerning-russias-implementation-of-its-wto

85 FR 56558 - Federal Acquisition Regulation: Maximizing Use of American-Made Goods, Products, and Materials
https://www.govinfo.gov/app/details/FR-2020-09-14/2020-20116

Establishment of Office of Trade and Manufacturing Policy
https://www.federalregister.gov/documents/2017/05/04/2017-09161/establishment-of-office-of-trade-and-manufacturing-policy

H.R.6758 - SUCCESS Act
https://www.congress.gov/bill/115th-congress/house-bill/6758

Reason 81. Stock Market Soars

Unemployment rate rises to record high 14.7 percent in April 2020
https://www.bls.gov/opub/ted/2020/unemployment-rate-rises-to-record-high-14-point-7-percent-in-april-2020.htm?view_full
Civilian unemployment rate
https://www.bls.gov/charts/employment-situation/civilian-unemployment-rate.htm

THE EMPLOYMENT SITUATION — AUGUST 2020
https://www.bls.gov/news.release/pdf/empsit.pdf

Dow Jones Industrial Average
https://www.wsj.com/market-data/quotes/index/DJIA/historical-prices

Employment Situation Archived News Releases
https://www.bls.gov/bls/news-release/empsit.htm#2018

Reason 82. Opportunity Zones

President Donald J. Trump Is Lifting Up and Driving New Prosperity in Previously Forgotten American Communities
https://trumpwhitehouse.archives.gov/briefings-statements/president-donald-j-trump-lifting-driving-new-prosperity-previously-forgotten-american-communities/

Executive Order on Targeting Opportunity Zones and Other Distressed Communities for Federal Site Locations
https://trumpwhitehouse.archives.gov/presidential-actions/executive-order-targeting-opportunity-zones-distressed-communities-federal-site-locations/

Remarks by President Trump at Signing of an Executive Order on the White House Hispanic Prosperity Initiative
https://trumpwhitehouse.archives.gov/briefings-statements/remarks-president-trump-signing-executive-order-white-house-hispanic-prosperity-initiative/

Executive Order on Establishing the White House Opportunity and Revitalization Council
https://trumpwhitehouse.archives.gov/presidential-actions/executive-order-establishing-white-house-opportunity-revitalization-council/

President Donald J. Trump Is Expanding Entrepreneurial Opportunity in Underserved Communities
https://trumpwhitehouse.archives.gov/briefings-statements/president-donald-j-trump-expanding-entrepreneurial-opportunity-underserved-communities/

Executive Order on Targeting Opportunity Zones and Other Distressed Communities for Federal Site Locations
https://trumpwhitehouse.archives.gov/presidential-actions/executive-order-targeting-opportunity-zones-distressed-communities-federal-site-locations/

Trump to Steer More Money to 'Opportunity Zones'
https://www.nytimes.com/2018/12/12/us/politics/trump-opportunity-zones-tax-cut.html?partner=bloomberg

What You Need to Know About Opportunity Zones
https://www.forbes.com/sites/morgansimon/2019/03/30/what-you-need-to-know-about-opportunity-zones/#103847ee6ae2

WTAS: Support for the Trump Administration's Approval of Opportunity Zones
https://trumpwhitehouse.archives.gov/briefings-statements/wtas-support-trump-administrations-approval-opportunity-zones/

List of Opportunity Zones by State
https://opportunitydb.com/location/

Trump Order Is Latest Effort to Bolster Opportunity Zones
https://news.bloombergtax.com/daily-tax-report/trump-order-is-latest-effort-to-bolster-opportunity-zones

Reason 83. Protecting Intellectual Property

Presidential Memorandum on the Actions by the United States Related to the Section 301 Investigation
https://trumpwhitehouse.archives.gov/presidential-actions/presidential-memorandum-actions-united-states-related-section-301-investigation/

President Donald J. Trump Is Protecting America From China's Efforts To Steal Technology And Intellectual Property
https://trumpwhitehouse.archives.gov/briefings-statements/president-donald-j-trump-protecting-america-chinas-efforts-steal-technology-intellectual-property/

President Trump Takes Action on Intellectual Property Rights
https://trumpwhitehouse.archives.gov/articles/president-trump-takes-action-intellectual-property-rights/

U.S. Intellectual Property Enforcement Coordinator
https://trumpwhitehouse.archives.gov/omb/office-u-s-intellectual-property-enforcement-coordinator-ipec/

Ensuring Safe & Lawful E-Commerce for US Consumers, Businesses, Government Supply Chains, and Intellectual Property Rights
https://trumpwhitehouse.archives.gov/presidential-actions/ensuring-safe-lawful-e-commerce-us-consumers-businesses-government-supply-chains-intellectual-property-rights/

DCPD-202000056 - Executive Order 13904-Ensuring Safe and Lawful E-Commerce for United States Consumers, Businesses, Government Supply Chains, and Intellectual Property Rights
https://www.govinfo.gov/app/details/DCPD-202000056

DCPD-201900203 - Memorandum on Combating Trafficking in Counterfeit and Pirated Goods
https://www.govinfo.gov/app/details/DCPD-201900203

The Cost of Malicious Cyber Activity to the U.S. Economy
https://trumpwhitehouse.archives.gov/wp-content/uploads/2018/02/The-Cost-of-Malicious-Cyber-Activity-to-the-U.S.-Economy.pdf

Reason 84. Companies Invest in U.S.

Ford cancels Mexico plant. Will create 700 U.S. jobs in 'vote of confidence' in Trump
https://money.cnn.com/2017/01/03/news/economy/ford-700-jobs-trump/

Charter promises Trump something new ($25-billion investment) and something old (20,000 jobs)
https://www.latimes.com/business/la-fi-trump-charter-jobs-20170324-story.html

Governor Abbott Joins President Trump For Charter Communications Jobs Announcement
https://gov.texas.gov/es/news/post/governor_abbott_joins_president_trump_for_charter_communications_jobs_annou

Toyota to invest $10 billion in U.S. over five years
https://www.reuters.com/article/us-usa-autoshow-toyota/toyota-to-invest-10-billion-in-u-s-over-five-years-idUSKBN14T1NN

Reason 85. Companies Expand Across U.S.

Amazon Selects New York City and Northern Virginia for New Headquarters
https://press.aboutamazon.com/news-releases/news-release-details/amazon-selects-new-york-city-and-northern-virginia-new

Retailers opening hundreds of new stores in 2018
https://www.businessinsider.com/retailers-opening-new-stores-this-year-2018-1

Amgen CEO Tells Trump the Company Plans to Hire 1,600 this Year
https://www.biospace.com/article/amgen-ceo-tells-b-trump-b-the-company-plans-to-hire-1-600-employees-this-year-/

Reason 86. Renewed Confidence in U.S. Industry

United States Consumer Sentiment
https://tradingeconomics.com/united-states/consumer-confidence

NAM Data & Research
https://www.nam.org/data-research/

Manufacturers' Outlook Survey
https://www.nam.org/manufacturers-outlook-survey/

Reason 87. Big Companies Repatriate Money to U.S.

Manufacturers bringing the most jobs back to America
https://www.usatoday.com/story/money/business/2018/06/28/manufacturers-bringing-most-jobs-back-to-america/36438051/

208

Reason 88. Time-Honored American Companies Come Home

Manufacturers bringing the most jobs back to America
https://www.usatoday.com/story/money/business/2018/06/28/
manufacturers-bringing-most-jobs-back-to-america/36438051/

Reason 89. Voluntary Minimum Wage Increases

Foxconn announces $10 billion investment in Wisconsin and up to 13,000 jobs
https://www.jsonline.com/story/news/2017/07/26/scott-walker-
heads-d-c-trump-prepares-wisconsin-foxconn-
announcement/512077001/

Intel Supports American Innovation with $7 Billion Investment in Next-Generation Semiconductor Factory in Arizona
https://newsroom.intel.com/news-releases/intel-supports-
american-innovation-7-billion-investment-next-generation-
semiconductor-factory-arizona/#gs.eh2nkz

Wells Fargo raises hourly minimum wage to $15, also to donate $400 million in 2018
https://www.marketwatch.com/story/wells-fargo-raises-hourly-
minimum-wage-to-15-also-to-donate-400-million-in-2018-
2017-12-20

Walmart is raising its minimum wage and handing out tax cut bonuses
https://money.cnn.com/2018/01/11/news/companies/walmart-
minimum-wage-increase/index.html

Intel Corp. Announces $7 Billion Investment in Arizona Plant
https://www.wsj.com/articles/intel-corp-announces-7-billion-
investment-in-arizona-plant-1486578589

Reason 90. Rebuilding Infrastructure

SECURING FEDERAL NETWORKS
https://www.cisa.gov/securing-federal-networks

Establishing Discipline and Accountability in the Environmental Review and Permitting Process for Infrastructure Projects
https://www.federalregister.gov/documents/2017/08/24/2017-18134/establishing-discipline-and-accountability-in-the-environmental-review-and-permitting-process-for

S. 496 (115th): A bill to repeal the rule issued by the Federal Highway Administration and the Federal Transit Administration entitled "Metropolitan Planning Organization Coordination and Planning Area Reform"
https://www.govtrack.us/congress/bills/115/s496/summary

Six Interior Infrastructure Projects that Benefit the Public
https://trumpwhitehouse.archives.gov/articles/6-interior-infrastructure-projects-benefit-public/

Reason 91. U.S. Protections

Presidential Executive Order 13799: Establishment of Presidential Advisory Commission on Election Integrity
https://www.dhs.gov/publication/executive-order-13799

EXECUTIVE ORDER ON STRENGTHENING THE CYBERSECURITY OF FEDERAL NETWORKS AND CRITICAL INFRASTRUCTURE
https://www.cisa.gov/executive-order-strengthening-cybersecurity-federal-networks-and-critical-infrastructure

Task Force on the United States Postal System
https://www.federalregister.gov/documents/2018/04/18/2018-
08272/task-force-on-the-united-states-postal-system
Executive Order on Addressing the Threat Posed by WeChat
https://trumpwhitehouse.archives.gov/presidential-
actions/executive-order-addressing-threat-posed-wechat/

Executive Order on Addressing the Threat Posed by TikTok
https://trumpwhitehouse.archives.gov/presidential-
actions/executive-order-addressing-threat-posed-tiktok/

*Order Regarding the Acquisition of Musical.ly by ByteDance
Ltd*
https://trumpwhitehouse.archives.gov/presidential-
actions/order-regarding-acquisition-musical-ly-bytedance-ltd/

The Cost of Malicious Cyber Activity to the U.S. Economy
https://trumpwhitehouse.archives.gov/wp-
content/uploads/2018/02/The-Cost-of-Malicious-Cyber-
Activity-to-the-U.S.-Economy.pdf

*CEA Report: The Cost of Malicious Cyber Activity to the U.S.
Economy*
https://trumpwhitehouse.archives.gov/articles/cea-report-cost-
malicious-cyber-activity-u-s-economy/

Reason 92. Tech Jobs Came Back

*Which manufacturers are bringing the most jobs back to
America?*
https://www.usatoday.com/story/money/business/2018/06/28/
manufacturers-bringing-most-jobs-back-to-america/36438051/

*Apple announces plans to repatriate billions in overseas cash,
says it will contribute $350 billion to the US economy over the
next 5 years*

https://www.cnbc.com/2018/01/17/apple-announces-350-billion-investment-20k-jobs-over-5-years.html

10 Companies That Are Bringing Jobs Back to America
https://investorplace.com/2017/01/10-companies-bringing-jobs-back-to-america/

7 Reasons Manufacturers Are Returning to the US
https://www.asme.org/topics-resources/content/7-reasons-manufacturers-are-returning-to-the-us

Reason 93. American Innovation

Executive Order on Maintaining American Leadership in Artificial Intelligence
https://trumpwhitehouse.archives.gov/presidential-actions/executive-order-maintaining-american-leadership-artificial-intelligence/

Establishment of the American Technology Council
https://www.federalregister.gov/documents/2017/05/03/2017-09083/establishment-of-the-american-technology-council

President Donald J. Trump is Standing Up for American Innovation
https://trumpwhitehouse.archives.gov/briefings-statements/president-donald-j-trump-standing-american-innovation/

Addressing China's Laws, Policies, Practices, and Actions Related to Intellectual Property, Innovation, and Technology
https://www.federalregister.gov/documents/2017/08/17/2017-17528/addressing-chinas-laws-policies-practices-and-actions-related-to-intellectual-property-innovation

Reason 94. Less Need for Public Assistance

SUPPLEMENTAL NUTRITION ASSISTANCE PROGRAM
https://fns-prod.azureedge.net/sites/default/files/resource-
files/34SNAPmonthly-7b.xls

SNAP Data Tables
https://www.fns.usda.gov/pd/supplemental-nutrition-
assistance-program-snap

Reason 95. Space Force

National Space Council Directives
https://www.space.commerce.gov/policy/national-space-
council-directives/

Reviving the National Space Council
https://www.federalregister.gov/documents/2017/07/07/2017-
14378/reviving-the-national-space-council

*President Donald J. Trump is Establishing America's Space
Force*
https://trumpwhitehouse.archives.gov/briefings-
statements/president-trump-establishing-americas-space-force/

*Presidential Executive Order on Reviving the National Space
Council*
https://trumpwhitehouse.archives.gov/presidential-
actions/presidential-executive-order-reviving-national-space-
council/

*Text of Space Policy Directive-4: Establishment of the United
States Space Force*
https://trumpwhitehouse.archives.gov/presidential-actions/text-
space-policy-directive-4-establishment-united-states-space-
force/

Memorandum on Space Policy Directive-5—Cybersecurity Principles for Space Systems
https://trumpwhitehouse.archives.gov/presidential-actions/memorandum-space-policy-directive-5-cybersecurity-principles-space-systems/

Reason 96. JFK Transparency

New Group of JFK Assassination Documents Available to the Public
https://www.archives.gov/press/press-releases/nr18-45

Reason 97. Solid Stability

Trump hosts leaders of Serbia, Kosovo for signing of historic agreement
https://nypost.com/2020/09/04/trump-hosts-serbia-kosovo-leaders-for-historic-deal-signing/

Trump nominated for second Nobel Peace Prize following Serbia-Kosovo deal
https://nypost.com/2020/09/11/donald-trump-nominated-for-second-nobel-peace-prize/

The 'Trump Doctrine' earns President third Nobel Peace Prize nomination
https://www.skynews.com.au/details/_6195238657001

Australian Law Professors Nominate Trump for Nobel Peace Prize for Third Time
https://blackchristiannews.com/2020/09/australian-law-professors-nominate-trump-for-nobel-peace-prize-for-third-time/

Trump gets third 2020 Nobel Peace Prize nomination
https://www.foxnews.com/politics/trump-third-nobel-nomination-doctrine

Reason 98. The Trump 2020 Second Term Agenda

TRUMP CAMPAIGN ANNOUNCES PRESIDENT TRUMP'S 2ND TERM AGENDA: FIGHTING FOR YOU!
https://www.donaldjtrump.com/media/trump-campaign-announces-president-trumps-2nd-term-agenda-fighting-for-you

Commitment to America
https://www.republicanleader.gov/issues/commitmenttoamcrica/

Reason 99. President Trump Does it for (Almost) Free

Confirmed: Donald Trump Says He Will Take $1 Salary as President
https://www.breitbart.com/politics/2016/11/13/confirmed-donald-trump-says-will-take-1-salary-president/

Donald Trump Donates Quarterly Salary to Repair National Monuments
https://www.breitbart.com/politics/2020/08/14/donald-trump-donates-quarterly-salary-to-repair-national-monuments/

Where Did President Trump Donate His Salary?
https://www.snopes.com/news/2019/12/13/president-trump-salary-donation/

3 U.S. Code § 102 - Compensation of the President
https://www.law.cornell.edu/uscode/text/3/102

Reason 100. President Trump Believes in America

President Donald J. Trump: Year One of Making America Great Again
https://trumpwhitehouse.archives.gov/briefings-statements/president-donald-j-trump-year-one-making-america-great/
Remarks by President Trump in Joint Address to Congress
https://trumpwhitehouse.archives.gov/briefings-statements/remarks-president-trump-joint-address-congress/